Collaborative
FamilyWork

About the author

Chris Trotter is Professor in Social Work at Monash University. He has an international reputation for his research on family work, offender supervision and pro-social modelling. He is author of *Working with Involuntary Clients* and *Helping Abused Children and their Families*, and his books have been translated into German, Japanese and Chinese.

CHRIS TROTTER

Collaborative FamilyWork

A practical guide to
working with families in
the human services

ALLEN&UNWIN
SYDNEY•MELBOURNE•AUCKLAND•LONDON

Allen & Unwin

83 Alexander Street
Crows Nest NSW 2065
Australia
Phone: (61 2) 8425 0100
Email: info@allenandunwin.com
Web: www.allenandunwin.com

Cataloguing-in-Publication details are available
from the National Library of Australia
www.trove.nla.gov.au

ISBN 978 1 74175 832 0

Set in 12/14.5pt Bembo by Post Pre-press Group, Australia
Printed by Hang Tai Printing Company Ltd

10 9 8 7 6 5 4 3 2 1

Contents

Figures

Acknowledgements

Many people have influenced the development of Collaborative Family Work. The book owes much to the ideas of the late William Reid on family problem-solving and task-centred casework and to the work of the late Don Andrews on pro-social modelling and other skills. I am particularly indebted to the human service professionals who have helped to develop the Collaborative Family Work model over the past 20 years. I make particular mention of Loretta Allen-Weinstein, Leonie Bender and the staff of Youth Justice in the Western Region New South Wales, Jane Christmas and Brian Heath from the probation service in the channel island of Jersey and Cath Powell, Charlene Periera and Matt Currie from the GRIPP program in the Dandenong Children's Court. Thanks go to Michael Clanchy who commented on an early draft of the book, Susie Costello and the reviewers who provided valuable comments on a later draft, and Lizzy Walton and Elizabeth Weiss from Allen & Unwin, who waited patiently for the book to be finished. Thanks to the editors Ann Lennox and Susan Jarvis and to Louise Oliaro and Tamara Thornton for their contribution to the case study transcripts. Thanks also to my department and colleagues at Monash University who allowed me the time to write. Finally, thank you to Joan and my family for their ongoing support.

For seminars on Collaborative Family Work, contact: christopher.trotter@monash.edu.

1

Introduction: Why Collaborative Family Work?

Sylvia works as a youth justice worker. She supervises young people who are placed on probation. Steve is 14 years old, and is one of her clients. He is on probation for stealing cars. He also has a problem with sniffing glue. Sylvia has worked with Steve for three months since he was placed on probation and has come to know him well. He has a long history of stealing cars and is due to return to court next week to face charges for another offence. He has a very poor record of school attendance and is pretty much illiterate. He has no real friends and most of his acquaintances are also school truants.

He lives with his father, Mario, his father's partner, Maria, and her two children, Emily, 14, and Jane, 11. Steve's mother died when he was 4 years old. He likes his father's partner but feels that she favours her own two children. Steve and his father don't get on well. They rarely talk to each other and Steve feels that his father does not like him. Sylvia has interviewed Mario on several occasions and she feels that his rejecting and authoritarian attitude to Steve is an important factor in Steve's behaviour. In fact, it is her view that one of the reasons why Steve steals cars is to get his father's attention. On several occasions after police have visited the house, Mario has told Steve to get out of the house and not come back. This has been followed by Steve getting into further trouble. On one occasion after he was told to leave, Steve broke into a house with some other young people and stole money and food.

Sylvia feels that Mario cares about Steve but does not know how to deal with his behaviour—harsh discipline is the only way he knows. Mario has acknowledged to Sylvia that it isn't working, but says that he can think of no other way of handling the situation. Steve talks about his father as if he is in awe of him. He talks about his father's work as a supervisor in an engineering shop that repairs ambulances. The ambulances must be maintained in perfect condition and only top-class mechanics can work in this field. He also talks about the times his father took him to the football, to the beach and so on.

Sylvia feels that she has done about as much as she can for this family. She has talked to Steve at length and she has talked to Mario and tried to persuade him to be more positive with Steve, and (to try) to let him know that he cares about him. She has even talked to Maria and asked her to encourage Mario to be more positive towards Steve. She feels that if she could get the relevant family members together—maybe Steve, Mario and Maria, or even just Steve and Mario—she could work through the issues more effectively. However, she feels that she does not have the skills or the confidence to work together with the family members to address the issues they are facing.

The aim of this book is to help professional workers like Sylvia to develop the skills and confidence to do this.

Andrea is a foster care worker. Sophia is 12 and has been in kinship foster care with her aunt, Stephanie, and Stephanie's partner, Huang, for three years. Sophia had been in several foster care placements before this; she had been happy with Stephanie and Huang until everything started to go downhill a few months ago. Stephanie rang Andrea, saying that things had deteriorated so much that they could no longer continue to foster Sophia. Her temper tantrums made them scared and they felt it was only a matter of time before she turned violent. They were also worried that their other two children were beginning to dislike Sophia. Andrea was very disappointed with the foster parents' attitude, mostly because it would be so difficult to place Sophia with another family. Sophia's mother was not an option—while she had some contact with Sophia, she continued to struggle with a mental illness and was not in a position to have her daughter with her. Earlier attempts to place Sophia with other relatives had failed.

Andrea understood the reluctance of the foster parents to keep Sophia with them; however, she could see that a move at this stage was not in Sophia's best interests, and she was worried that she would ultimately end up homeless. Andrea attempted to do some mediation with the three of them. She even tried involving Naomi,

Stephanie's 16-year-old daughter. However, this did not seem to help and Andrea felt that she did not really know how to tackle working with the family group.

In both of these situations, the professional worker feels that working with the family group may be the best way to deal with the issues facing the family and the worker. However, in each case, even though the workers have professional qualifications, they do not feel equipped to work with the family group through a series of family counselling sessions. This book aims to help them do this. It aims to help social workers, welfare workers, psychologists, school counsellors and others in the human services to work through a series of family sessions with client families.

This chapter introduces the Collaborative Family Work model, discusses the aims of the book and clarifies the terminology relating to family work, family therapy, family counselling and family mediation. It identifies situations where human service workers work with families, and discusses some of the benefits and difficulties of working with the family group rather than, or as well as, working with family members individually. It also discusses situations where family work may not be appropriate—for example, with families who are experiencing domestic violence or child sexual abuse.

Why Collaborative Family Work?

There have been many books published on working with families. There are general books on family therapy and there are books on specific forms of family therapy—including psychodynamic, structural, experiential and behavioural models. There are books on narrative and solution-focused family work and books on problem-solving with families. So why is there a need for another book on working with families? There is a need for *Collaborative Family Work* because there are few if any other books like it. It differs from other books on working with families because it focuses on families in the social services and criminal justice systems, many of whom are involuntary clients. It presents a model that has been developed for use with young offenders and their families, with families in the child protection system, with young people who are homeless, with families of children referred to school welfare staff, with family members with learning disability or acquired brain injury, and with family members with drug and alcohol addictions. It has been developed and used with families experiencing poverty and with families from many different backgrounds, including Australian Indigenous families.

This is a practical book that provides the tools for professional workers in the social services or youth justice systems to work through a series of sessions with family members. Many family therapy models require years of training for practitioners to develop expertise. However, research and experience with the model presented in this book suggest that professional workers can successfully apply the model by following the steps as they are outlined in this book. Similarly, students in social work, welfare, psychology, counselling or other human services courses can develop expertise in working with family groups by using this book as a basis.

A particular strength of the Collaborative Family Work model is that it is readily understood by clients who may not be well educated or particularly articulate. Family members can understand and follow the steps in the model during sessions with their workers, and they can use the steps in the model to solve problems for themselves. It teaches skills that family members can use outside of family work sessions.

The model is presented in user-friendly language that aims to be as straightforward as possible. Nevertheless, the application of the model requires skill and contains complexities that may not be apparent on the first reading. Experience has shown that while professional workers in the social services can work successfully with the model with minimal training or experience, over time they learn to operate with increasing degrees of expertise. In other words, the model can readily be understood by workers and clients and inexperienced workers can work successfully with the model; however, with experience workers can become more expert and more successful in its application.

There are a number of commercial family work models available for use by professional workers. Some of these involve a process of training and certification. The model presented in this book does not require such a process. This is not to say that training and ongoing supervision will not enhance the skills of those offering Collaborative Family Work. In fact, when organisations have implemented the model, it has been most successful when initial and ongoing training has been offered followed by professional supervision or debriefing after each family work session. However, it is acknowledged that many professional workers work with families on a regular or an irregular basis, and often do not have the opportunity to access specific training or debriefing. Those workers can benefit from the knowledge offered in this book. By following the steps presented, they can successfully undertake work with family groups. They can use the expertise that they have developed in working with individuals and apply that expertise to work with families.

Collaborative Family Work is an evidence-based model. There are, of course, many books on work with families that are evidence-based. Like them, this book operates from a paradigm that focuses primarily on practices that are supported by research findings and consistent with established theories. I have addressed the issues surrounding evidence-based practice in earlier books (Trotter 2004, 2006), and it is acknowledged that there are arguments for and against evidence-based practice. Nevertheless, this book is firmly rooted in the evidence-based paradigm. At the same time, it acknowledges the importance of critical and reflective practice, as discussed in Chapter 2.

Family work, family therapy, family counselling and family mediation

This book is about working with families who have problems. It is about how a professional human services worker can undertake a series of family sessions with a family with a view to assisting them with their problems. It presents a problem-solving model for working with families. While the term 'family work' is used throughout this book, many of the skills that can be learnt from the book might also be described as family therapy, mediation or counselling skills.

Family therapy generally refers to long-term interventions with specifically trained family therapists. The formal definitions of family therapy tend to be general. The UK Association for Family Therapy and Systemic Practice suggests that:

> Family Therapists help family members find constructive ways to help each other. They work in ways that acknowledge the contexts of people's families and other

relationships, sharing and respecting individuals' different perspectives, beliefs, views and stories, and exploring possible ways forward. (<www.familytherapy.org.uk>)

The Association acknowledges that family therapists may have varying qualifications, some with little or no formal training (Stratton 2005). Family therapy may take place in one session or over several years.

The term 'family counselling' is sometimes used to describe work done with families following divorce and separation, and is often offered through the legal system when there are issues relating to the care of children. One definition includes:

> Family counselling is defined as a process in which a family counsellor helps one or more people to deal with personal or interpersonal issues relating to marriage, separation or divorce, including issues relating to the care of children.
> (Attorney-General's Department 2007: 2)

Family mediation is also often described in a legal context. The Legal Services Commission of South Australia (2011) refers to mediation as a 'form of dispute resolution where an impartial third party helps communication and negotiations between the parties, but does not decide the dispute.' In other words, family mediation tries to reach agreement between people—often between separating couples—about issues which they cannot agree on.

The Collaborative Family Work model for working with families presented in this book is more in line with definitions of family therapy. Some professional workers who make use of the Collaborative Family Work model describe themselves as family therapists. However, as discussed earlier, many who use the model are not specialist family therapists but workers in child protection, juvenile justice, schools or family-support agencies who use elements of family therapy in their work. The term 'family work' is used in this book because it is a more low-key term than 'family therapy', it is less associated with illness or dysfunction, and it is more readily accepted by the clients with whom it is most often used.

What is a family?

Families can be defined in many ways. Gill Barnes (1984:10) refers to the traditional view of family as 'the primary social group into which individuals are born and upon which they initially depend for nurture'. Faith Robertson Elliot (1986: 4) suggests that family is widely seen as a 'group based on marriage and biological parenthood, as sharing a common residence and as united by ties of affection', but then refers to the complexities of defining families. More recent publications have defined families more in terms of a system. Herbert and Irene Goldenberg (2008: 1) suggest that each family may be considered a 'natural sustained social system with properties all its own—one that has attained a set of rules, is replete with assigned and ascribed roles for its members, has an organised power structure, has developed intricate and overt forms of communication'.

Other texts have discussed definitions of families in more detail and it is not necessary to dwell on detailed definitions for the purposes of this book. Suffice to say that families come in many forms, and definitions may vary between cultures. For example, American and British people tend to focus on nuclear families, whereas Afro-American and

Australian Aboriginal families are more focused on a wider network of relatives and community members.

This book adopts a broad definition of families. Families may include members who have no blood relationship with other members—for example, in cases of adoption or foster care; they may include members who have no legal relationship with other members—for example, cohabiting couples; and they may include same-sex partners. Some people who live in close relationships may not constitute families from a traditional viewpoint; however, they may share many of the characteristics of families—for example, a young person who lives with the family of a friend, an ex-prisoner who is provided with accommodation by a family following release from prison, a congregrate care facility where 'house parents' care for the children, two friends who have lived together for many years or a small group of disabled people who live together and support each other. These people share some, if not all, of the characteristics referred to by Herbert and Irene Goldenberg (2008).

Rather than struggle with definitions of family, in this book we are more concerned with whether or not a family work intervention might be appropriate. Family interventions may be suitable for any situation where 'two or more people have a close or important personal interaction'—this becomes the definition of family for the purposes of this book.

For example, it may be appropriate to use the skills and practices offered in this book with groups who may not traditionally be described as families. Let us take the example of a young person who, following his release from prison, finds accommodation with a couple who have volunteered to support ex-prisoners through a prisoner support service.

The young person's parole officer feels that the accommodation is helpful, has a stabilising effect on the young person and has helped to keep him away from his criminal mates. After a period of time, difficulties develop in the relationship between the young person and the couple, and the accommodation arrangement looks like it may break down. In this situation, it may be appropriate for the parole officer, or another professional worker, to work with those involved to resolve their differences. The skills of working with families developed in this book are relevant to this process.

Do family interventions work?

This book is based on the assumption that working with families leads to good outcomes for family members. These may include reduced offending, reduced child abuse, reduced drug use, reduced homelessness or truancy, or improved family relationships. There is evidence that work with families does, in fact, lead to good outcomes. Some of this research is outlined below.

In a review of 'outcome research in family therapy', Eia Asen (2002) refers to major systemic approaches to work with families, including strategic, Milan systemic, narrative, psychoeducational and behavioural, although she acknowledges that practitioners in public welfare situations often use a mixture of approaches. She refers to a number of meta-analyses, including controlled trials, and to individual studies about services, which point to the effectiveness of systemic family work. She refers to positive outcomes in conduct problems in children, drug and alcohol misuse in adolescents and adults, childhood asthma, enuresis and soiling, behaviour problems, eating disorders, psychotic illnesses and mood disorders.

A review by Stratton (2005) came to a similar conclusion, arguing that Systemic Family Therapy is effective for a wide range of issues such as child conduct and mood disorders, eating disorders, drug misuse, schizophrenia, depression and chronic physical illness. Alan Carr (2011), in a more recent review, argues on the basis of the available research that 25 to 75 per cent of people benefit from marital and family therapy. In particular, he suggests that the evidence is very strong for the effectiveness of family therapy in treating externalised behaviour problems and disruptive behaviour disorders, although he acknowledges that most of the research has been conducted on cognitive behavioural, psycho-educational and structural-strategic therapeutic approaches.

There is considerable evidence in support of cognitive behavioural interventions with families. A summary is provided in Corcoran (2000). Cognitive programs help people to change distorted thinking. For example, when a child cries a mother may believe that the child is doing it deliberately to upset her. Cognitive interventions would challenge this thinking to help the mother understand that the child is crying because he or she is hungry or distressed, or wanting attention, and that the crying is not personally directed against the mother. This, in turn, can help the mother to react in an understanding rather than a hostile manner. Cognitive interventions of this nature may be delivered to parents on an individual basis or with family groups.

Family interventions using cognitive behavioural principles have been shown to be effective in criminal justice settings. Sexton and Turner (2010) found a reduction in recidivism of young offenders offered Functional Family Therapy, a systems cognitive behavioural approach (described in Chapter 2), compared with young offenders offered probation alone. They found a statistically significant reduction of 35 per cent in felonies and a 30 per cent reduction in violent crime one year after treatment. However, they found that the benefits of the family intervention were only present if the family workers adhered to the Functional Family Therapy model.

The studies of Functional Family Therapy are of particular interest because the model has many similarities to Collaborative Family Work. It is a short-term behavioural approach using modelling and reinforcement, as well as contingency contracting and exchanges of tasks between family members.

This work built on earlier research by Alexander and Parsons (1973). While this research was done a long time ago, it provides an excellent illustration of the potential for family work to make a difference. The study was undertaken with a group of minor 'delinquents'. These young people (aged from 13 to 16) had been arrested or detained by a juvenile court for offences such as running away, truanting, shoplifting or possession of soft drugs. Families were randomly assigned to one of four treatment conditions.

One of the treatment options was a precursor to Functional Family Therapy. The study compared three control groups to the treatment group: a client-centred family group, which focused on client and family feelings; a psychodynamic group sponsored by the Mormon Church with a focus on insight; and a group that received no treatment. Reoffence rates after six to eighteen months were 50 per cent in the no-treatment group, 47 per cent in the client-centred group, 73 per cent in the psychodynamic group and 26 per cent in the short-term family behavioural treatment group. Subsequent studies using Functional Family Therapy—in some instances, with more serious young offenders—found similar positive results with sizeable reductions in reoffence rates (Alexander et al. 1978; Barton et al. 1985; Gordon et al. 1988; Gordon & Arbuthnot 1990; Sexton & Alexander 2002b).

A review of research on Functional Family Therapy (Sexton & Alexander 2002a) suggests that in addition to its impact on reoffending, it is effective with young people with problems relating to substance abuse, mental health, maltreatment and neglect, and sexual offences. Further, it maintains its benefits even after five years, and it shows benefits for other family members—particularly younger siblings.

Similar positive outcomes have also been seen with the more broadly based multi-systemic therapy. This is an intensive intervention approach that targets all aspects of a young person's situation, including parent education, family therapy, interactions with outside agencies, peers, schooling and neighbourhood support. Once again, the research points to significant improvements in problems related to school attendance, rearrest rates, drug use, maltreatment and rates of institutionalisation (Sexton & Alexander 2002a; Perkins-Dock 2001). It seems that family work may be particularly effective when combined with other effective treatments or interventions.

There is evidence that the individual qualities and skills of the workers who deliver family work may be just as important as the model that is used. Blow, Sprenkle and Davis (2007) argue, based on a review of research, that there are certain core skills that lead to positive outcomes, regardless of the intervention model. They refer to 'alliance building, client engagement, hope and expectancy generation, relational conceptualization of problems, changing meanings, and matching to the unique worlds of clients as common factors which relate to good outcomes regardless of the model used' (2007: 311). This is similar to the argument presented in *Working with Involuntary Clients* (Trotter 2006) that certain worker skills and practices, role clarification and pro-social modelling, for example, are consistently related to positive outcomes for clients.

Generally, the research suggests that when family interventions with disadvantaged families are implemented as planned, they are effective—particularly those using cognitive behavioural and systemic approaches. These interventions are, however, more likely to be successful if the worker has strong interpersonal skills and can build an alliance with the family.

When is it appropriate to work with families?

There are situations when it is better to work with the family group than to work individually. Sometimes it is only when family members are brought together with a professional that issues can be aired in a rational manner and realistic decisions can be made.

To take one real-life example where family work led to an outcome that could not have been achieved through individual work with family members, a 13-year-old girl, Amy, was placed in the care of the state following her violent behaviour at home and other risky behaviours including illegal drug use. She was subsequently placed in several supported accommodation arrangements, most recently in an adolescent unit catering for young women experiencing severe behaviour difficulties. However, the unit staff members were unable to cope with her violence towards staff and other residents, and she was asked to leave. Her mother had consistently said that she would not have Amy return to live with her under any circumstances, and she persisted in this view even though the case manager felt that this was the best option for Amy.

The case manager was able to persuade the mother to meet with her and Amy prior to her discharge from her accommodation. This was on the understanding that Amy could not return home to live. The meeting was only to talk about possible options. During the first meeting, the mother and Amy agreed to be involved in a series of collaborative family work sessions on the continued understanding that Amy would not be returning to live with her mother. As the sessions progressed, Amy and her mother began to develop a greater appreciation of each other's situations and of the limited options available to Amy. The mother then suggested that Amy could come home on a trial basis and under certain conditions. Amy subsequently returned to live with her mother, and continued to live with her on an ongoing basis. The case manager met with them on several more occasions to deal with issues as they arose. In this instance, it is clear that Amy would not have returned home without the Collaborative Family Work sessions. It is unlikely that such an outcome would have been achieved if the case manager had worked with the family members individually.

There are many other situations when family work may be the most appropriate and best way to deal with a particular situation. It seems reasonable to say that if there is a problem within the family and family members agree to work together, family work is likely to be an appropriate method unless there are contra-indications. Some of these are set out below.

When is it not appropriate to work with families?

There are clearly occasions when it is not appropriate to work with families. The approach to working with families advocated in this book is based on a degree of equality existing among family members, as well as the capacity for family members to participate in a group discussion. This is not, of course, to suggest that only those families who get on well and are without conflict are suitable for family work. On the contrary, most of the therapeutic or counselling work undertaken with family groups involves family members who have poor communication, and interactions characterised by frequent conflict. Nevertheless, some capacity to communicate between family members is necessary to carry out a Collaborative Family Work intervention.

Family work with the perpetrator of sexual abuse and the victim of that abuse in the same room at the same time is inappropriate. It is unlikely that family work would be appropriate with the perpetrator and the victim of domestic violence. In these situations it is likely that the victim would feel intimidated and unable to speak freely in family work sessions.

Similarly, it may be difficult for some family members to participate in a meaningful way in family work if one member of the family is dominating and overbearing. It may also be difficult to work effectively with families where the cultural expectation is that children will behave in certain ways, particularly if the cultural 'norm' is not questioned by other family members. For example, parents may have rigid expectations about their children having arranged marriages, despite living in a new culture that views individual choice in marriage as a basic human right. In a situation such as this,

the worker may take the view that family work is not likely
to help because of the intransigent position of the parents.

Nevertheless, there may be occasions where family work
is appropriate despite the presence of an overbearing family
member. Let us take a similar example to the one relating to
Steve, raised earlier. In this real-life case example, the worker
had skills and confidence in working with families.

> Joe, a 14 year old boy, had committed a series of crimi-
> nal offences and was placed on probation. Joe lived with
> his mother and father and two brothers. The probation
> officer undertook an assessment of the family situation
> and came to the view that the young person's rejection
> by and limited engagement with his father were factors
> in his criminal offending. The probation officer felt that
> the aggressive and domineering behaviour of the father
> provided a poor role model for Joe. Joe's mother also
> regretted the poor relationship Joe had with his father.
> The probation officer believed that there would be ben-
> efits if the father could be helped to understand that his
> rejection of Joe had led his son to some of his anti-social
> behaviour and that a more productive relationship might
> lead to improving his behaviour.
>
> In this instance, the probation officer took the view
> that family work was suitable if Joe, his mother and his
> father were agreeable. The probation officer was then
> able to 'sell' the idea of family work to Joe, the father and
> the mother. Joe saw the potential advantages of a better
> relationship with his father—in fact, he was desperate
> for such an outcome; the father was agreeable because
> he was persuaded by his wife, and because he accepted
> that it may help to improve Joe's behaviour.

Once they began the family work using the Collaborative Family Work model, the structure of the model allowed for a modification of the father's dominant behaviour and provided an opportunity for Joe to talk to and be listened to by his father.

In another example, a dominating father chose not to be involved because he felt uncomfortable with the equitable nature of the model, yet after some weeks he decided he would come along as an observer. This was discussed with him by the workers, and they agreed along with the family that he could sit in on the sessions but not contribute on the understanding that he complied with each of the other ground rules—for example, not raising issues discussed in the sessions outside the sessions. After attending two sessions on this basis, he asked whether he could participate, and the workers felt that his dominating attitudes were subsequently broken down by the process of the family work.

In a number of the collaborative work interventions in which I have been involved, issues of sexual abuse have arisen during the sessions that were not apparent at the time of the initial assessment. On several occasions, the family work ceased and the victim of sexual abuse was referred for individual counselling or to child protection. On some occasions, police charges were laid. While it is not appropriate to bring victims and perpetrators of sexual abuse together for family work, when this occurs in situations where the abuse is hidden, the family work may act as a protection for the victim because it can help to bring the issue into the open.

The age of the children may also be a factor in determining suitability for family work. In Collaborative Family Work, children of all ages have been in the room while the sessions have taken place. A child of 7, for example, may not be able to participate meaningfully in the discussions but may gain something from hearing the conversations and from observing a more cordial and collaborative interaction between family members than they might hear under normal circumstances. While participation in family work requires some ability to follow a discussion, there are nevertheless many examples of successful Collaborative Family Work interventions with family members with intellectual disability, mental illness and histories of drug addiction. Generally speaking, if family members are agreeable and there are no contra-indications, family work is likely to be suitable.

Assessing suitability for family work

This leads to a discussion about the assessment process. As discussed above, sexual abuse in particular may be a closely guarded secret within a family. Despite all the best efforts of the professionals involved, an initial assessment may not identify the presence of the abuse. Similarly, domestic violence may be unspoken. In one case example, two human service workers worked with a man and his partner using the Collaborative Family Work model for six consecutive sessions, and it was not until the seventh session that the physical violence the man was perpetrating on his partner became apparent to the workers.

Nevertheless, it is important that family work is preceded by a thorough assessment. In most cases in work with families in the welfare system, there will be a primary client. This client may be a child protection client, a probation client, a client of a school welfare service, a client of a drug and alcohol service or a client in the mental health system. In most cases, the worker will carry out a detailed assessment as part of the expectations of the agency for which they work. This will include gathering information about the client's school/employment, peer group, drug use, mental health, finances and other issues. It will also involve discussions about the client's family. If the family members fight with each other, the worker might ask how they fight and whether the fighting is physical.

In making a decision about the suitability for family work, certain criteria may be used:

- Are there reasons why this client or the client family may be unsuitable for family work?

- Do the problems or issues faced by the client relate to the family interaction?

- Does the client have a sound knowledge of what is involved?

- Does the client agree to be involved?

- Is there at least one other family member who agrees to be involved?

- Do other family members who will be involved understand the nature of the family work?

- Are the family members and the worker/s who agree to be involved available on a regular basis to participate in family sessions, in the worker's office, the family home or elsewhere?

- Are there cultural impediments to Collaborative Family Work that cannot be overcome by preparing family members and developing ground rules?

The model

The Collaborative Family Work model presented in this book contains six basic steps. As discussed earlier, the terminology used to describe the model aims as far as possible to make the model accessible to clients and the six steps are described in user-friendly language as set out in the box. The acronym RIDGES in Figure 1.1 is sometimes used to describe the steps in the model.

Figure 1.1: RIDGES model

1. **R**ules—set ground rules.
2. **I**dentify issues that we would like to change.
3. **D**ecide what to work on first.
4. **G**oals—what do we want to achieve?
5. **E**xplore the issue in more detail.
6. **S**trategies/activities—work out ways of achieving the goals.

Throughout this book, I have tried to keep the language as accessible and readable as possible. I have done this for two reasons. First, I am trying to outline a model that clients can understand. Hopefully some clients of the human services will be able to read the book and benefit from it. Second, in the direct practice work that I have done in over 20 years in adult probation, juvenile justice, child protection, mental health and foster care, and in the research projects I have carried out on work with individuals and families, it has always been apparent that translating the knowledge learnt from texts to practice situations is difficult. It is difficult to remember what has been learnt and it is difficult to apply that knowledge.

There has been some work done on the concept of therapeutic integrity in work in criminal justice (Andrews & Dowden 2005), as well as a number of studies that have examined the skills workers use in their direct practice work in criminal justice and child protection (Bourgeon et al. 2010; Robinson et al. 2011; Trotter 2004; Trotter & Evans 2012). Theses studies suggest that workers often do not use basic skills in interviews. The use of measurable goals is infrequent, for example. I am hoping that the straightforward and easily remembered structure of the Collaborative Family Work model presented in this book can help to address this issue. There is sufficient complexity in family structures and family interactions without adding another layer in the form of an intervention model.

The structure of the book

Chapter 2 outlines a number of traditional and recent family therapy models. It briefly outlines models including trans-generational, experiential, structural, strategic, Milan systemic, cognitive behavioural, functional, narrative and solution-focused. It also comments on the relevance of critical and reflective practice to work with families.

Chapter 3 explains the background to the Collaborative Family Work model. It comments on elements of the model, including co-counselling, pro-social modelling, rating scales, supervision and debriefing. It then outlines the steps in the model.

Chapter 4 focuses on preparing families for family work and developing ground rules in the first session. Family members are often resistant to family counselling or family therapy. Sometimes one family member will seek assistance, but other family members are reluctant to be involved. On other occasions, family members may agree to be involved; however, they may have misconceptions about how the sessions will be conducted and their role in the process. Preparing family members for family work involves helping them to understand what will occur in the sessions, the extent to which discussions will be confidential, and what happens if the sessions become too stressful, if some family members choose not to attend or if one family member is too dominant. The chapter then focuses on working with family members in the initial session, and outlines a process for developing ground rules for the conduct of the sessions.

Chapter 5 continues the description of the steps in the Collaborative Family Work model. It discusses reviewing the previous session and moving on to problem identification. It outlines the procedure for identifying issues as family members see them, and discusses some of the issues faced by workers: What if clients don't identify the real issues? What does focusing on the here and now mean? How do you incorporate strengths?

Chapter 6 considers what to work on first, and suggests that workers and family members should focus on issues that are solvable, ethical, related to the reason the client is a client, and practical. It then discusses setting goals that are achievable, measurable and agreed to by all family members. The overlap between long- and short-term goals, and between goals and strategies, is discussed so workers can help family members to be as clear as possible about what they want to achieve.

Chapter 7 outlines problem exploration and the development of strategies. The strategies or tasks, as they are sometimes referred to, have been divided into session-based facilitative strategies, home-based facilitative strategies, problem-related session strategies and problem–related home strategies. This is followed by a discussion about addressing obstacles to the implementation of strategies, the need for strategies to fit with other services and the need for them to be culturally appropriate.

Chapter 8 focuses on ongoing review of the family work sessions and concluding the intervention. It discusses strategies to maintain what has been gained, and refers to ways in which family work interventions can be evaluated. It finishes with a real-life case study that illustrates each of the stages of the model.

2
Family work models and theories

Family therapy has a long history. However, it is not the intention of this book to provide a detailed description of the history of family work or to provide detailed descriptions of family therapy models. This has been done elsewhere—for example, in the detailed work of Irene and Herbert Goldenberg (2008). The focus of this chapter is on those components of family therapy that are relevant to the Collaborative Family Work model presented in this book.

This chapter focuses on some of the major family therapies carried out with family groups—in other words, with at least two family members. There are a number of ways of working with families that are not strictly family work or family therapy, so they are not addressed in this book—for example, parent training, which teaches parents parenting skills; family group conferencing, which is often used as a decision-making process regarding the placement of children or to assist in sentencing of young offenders; and multisystemic therapy, which uses family problem-solving as one component of a multi-faceted intervention with families.

The chapter begins with a description of the traditional therapies—psychodynamic, intergenerational, structural and strategic—and then moves on to examine the more recent approaches, such as cognitive behavioural, solution-focused and narrative therapies. The similarities to and differences from Collaborative Family Work are discussed in relation to each approach.

The traditional therapies

Sigmund Freud laid the foundations of psychodynamic theory in the early twentieth century. Freud believed, based on his work as a psychiatrist, that the early years of family life were highly influential in the development of the adult personality (Freud 1938). The early years can influence the development of healthy functioning or mental illness, as people struggle to deal with messages from their childhood. These messages are unconscious and may be influenced by three forces: the id, which is instinctive—mostly sexual and survival drives; the ego, which is adult and rational; and the superego, which exerts a controlling or moralistic force on the actions of individuals.

While Freud acknowledged the importance of family in human development, he did not advocate working with the family group, and preferred to work with individuals. Nevertheless, subsequent theorists and family therapists have used the principles of Freud's teachings in the development of family therapy models, as discussed later in this chapter. The particular relevance of Freud's work to Collaborative Family Work is his acknowledgement that many of the decisions people make and many of the thoughts they have formed at an unconscious level are influenced by past experiences. Also relevant is the notion that people may use psychological defence mechanisms to maintain irrational thoughts and beliefs. To take an example, a father who has been brought up, through a long-term process of modelling and reinforcement by his own parents, to believe that men should be in charge of the family, may continue to believe in his superior role in the family by virtue of being male. This may be at an unconscious level, and the father may have difficulty seeing any other point of view.

Collaborative Family Work is informed by an awareness of the notion that family members may be following particular roles because that is what their parents did. It is based on the assumption that breaking down entrenched beliefs and defences that have stemmed from childhood can be a complex process.

Transgenerational models

Many of the early models of family therapy were influenced by the psychoanalytic tradition. Transgenerational Family Therapy is based on the belief that family dysfunction often has its origins in family history. Murray Bowen (1978) refers to a family systems model, suggesting that family emotional systems may extend across several generations. He recommends using genograms to plot the family relationship system, suggesting that if people do not differentiate themselves from their family of origin, they continue to be tied to those patterns of functioning and they may marry people who have a similar lack of differentiation from their family of origin. In other words, the family emotional system perpetuates itself.

Transgenerational Family Therapy helps family members to differentiate from their families. It aims to help family members to develop a sense of fairness and trust rather than feelings of indebtedness and secrecy between family members, to help family members to take responsibility for their own thoughts and feelings, and to distinguish these from those of other family members. It examines long-term feelings of grievance, particularly the feelings that one person owes something to another family member. Transgenerational Family Therapists try to build on the sense of caring that family members have for each other.

While Collaborative Family Work has a conscious focus on the 'here and now' rather than past family conflicts and issues, it nevertheless makes use of a number of the principles of Transgenerational Family Therapy. While genograms are not generally used in Collaborative Family Work to trace family structures from previous generations, they are often used to help workers understand the structure of the family and to decide who is most appropriate to involve in family work.

The concept of intergenerational family patterns is relevant to work in human services, the field in which Collaborative Family Work is most commonly used. This is particularly so in justice settings, where young people may begin to develop a criminal identity from an early age through interaction with family members with criminal histories. In fact, there is evidence that as many as 60 per cent of males with a convicted father, and as many as 30 per cent of males with a convicted grandfather, may be convicted of a criminal offence (Goodwin & Davis 2011). Such patterns are also particularly relevant to work in child protection, where child-rearing practices may be passed through cultures and generations, with disproportionate representation of some minority groups in child protection systems around the world.

Nevertheless, while it is important that workers using the Collaborative Family Work model have an understanding of the nature of intergenerational and cultural learning, in practice the focus is on the 'here and now', and there are few instances when intergenerational work is done unless it is raised specifically by family members or there are current issues between family members from different generations.

Experiential Family Therapy

Experiential Family Therapy, developed by Virginia Satir (Satir et al. 1991) and Carl Whitaker (Whitaker & Bumberry 1988), is not driven by a particular theory but is focused on the potential of the relationship with the therapist to help family members to develop insight into their family relationships. Greater self-awareness, it is argued, can lead to greater levels of choice and improved levels of functioning. The therapist helps family members to analyse their underlying feelings, to communicate honestly and openly with each other, and to develop self-esteem through a focus on positives rather than negatives. The therapist tries to change repetitive communication styles with a focus on genuineness, avoiding secrets and unlocking defensiveness. Family members are encouraged to free themselves to express their innermost thoughts and feelings. Experiential Family Therapy is a flexible way of working, and the content of sessions varies according to the needs of the family and the focus of the individual therapist.

This approach does not use a specific structure. It focuses on the subjective needs of family members and the subjective judgements of the therapist. In this way, it is very different from Collaborative Family Work, which asks the workers to work through specific steps and activities. Collaborative

Family Work accepts that certain defence mechanisms and family secrets may be too difficult for family members to deal with, and it promotes the idea of allowing participants to move at their own pace. It asks participants to control their emotions and not to say hurtful things to each other, even if they may be genuine. It is cautious about the notion of building self-esteem as an objective because for some family members their self-esteem may be derived from their position as the dominant person in the family, or in some cases from their pro-criminal identity. On the other hand, Collaborative Family Work—like Experiential Family Therapy—asks family members to focus on positives, albeit only when those positives are of a pro-social nature, and to try to understand each other's points of view.

Structural Family Therapy

Structural Family Therapy (Minuchin 1974) focuses on family structures, including family sub-systems, family boundaries and coalitions. Families may be problematic if they are enmeshed—in other words, family members do not differentiate themselves from the family and family boundaries are rigid. They may also be dysfunctional if, rather than being enmeshed, they are disengaged from each other.

Structural Family Therapy works from the premise that healthy families have clear parent–child boundaries. They are not too rigid but also not too diffuse. Parents should fulfil their role as carers and decision-makers for their children, and children should carry out a role that is appropriate. Where children take on roles as substitute parents or where children and parents do not respect certain boundaries, this can lead to family problems. Similarly, when coalitions develop between family members—coalitions that may exclude other family members—this may also lead to unsatisfactory and unhealthy family relationships. For example, a young person might develop a very close relationship with their father in which the father confides in the young person about problems he is having with the young person's mother. This may leave the mother isolated and compromise the relationship between the young person and their mother.

The aim of Structural Family Therapy is to help families to develop more functional structures. Therapists try to help mothers and fathers and children to adopt roles and boundaries that are appropriate. In doing this, the therapist explores the family rules and patterns. Reframing may be used to help family members to understand another point of view. For example, if a young person is staying away from home a lot and this is upsetting his parents, the worker might reframe this into the young person seeking independence from the family and wanting to grow up. The therapist might help the parents to develop family rules that allow for more independence for the young person. Structural Family Therapists may also act out conflicts in sessions so that the therapist can show family members alternative ways of interacting.

Structural Family Therapy is clearly different from Collaborative Family Work inasmuch as it does not present a step-by-step method of working with a family. It is also different because Collaborative Family Work tries to avoid as far as possible making assumptions or assessments about the nature of individual family systems and boundaries. Rather, it aims to coach family members towards a method of interacting in ways that meet their needs. Nevertheless, it does make some assumptions about things that should be encouraged in family work. In particular, it encourages a focus on promoting pro-social activities (e.g. mixing with non-criminal peer groups or not using excessive physical discipline). It may also work to break down family coalitions where these are identified as an issue for one or more family members. Reframing techniques are an important part of Collaborative Family Work, and are used routinely in the model. Similarly, the concept of re-enactment or role-play is commonly used as a strategy to address difficulties in communication between family members. Family members may, for example, role-play a typical argument and can then be encouraged by the worker to use a different method of communicating.

Strategic Family Therapy
Strategic Family Therapy has its origins in the 1950s. Unlike many of the psycho-dynamic and experiential approaches, it focuses specifically on the presenting problem, or symptom. It is particularly associated with the work of Jay Haley and Cloe Madanes (Haley 1987; Madanes & Haley 1977) and Gregory Bateson (1979). It is a short-term model that focuses on the symptom without seeking to find a 'real' underlying problem. It assumes that family problems are maintained because of the ways in which family members consistently interact. The therapist gathers information from the family members about the presenting problems and what they have done to address them in the past. The therapist then develops activities for the family to address the problems. This can involve helping the family members to understand repetitive patterns and teaching family members to avoid attempting solutions that have failed in the past.

This approach uses certain concepts such as 'paradoxical communication', whereby family members can be asked to repeat the undesired behaviour. For example, the family members are invited to continue arguing over how often one family member should clean up their bedroom. This is aimed to show the family members that they can control how they interact, and therefore can change it. The concept of 're-labelling' involves naming an undesirable comment or task in a more positive way—for example, cleaning up the room might be re-labelled as making the room comfortable enough to entertain friends when they visit. Strategic Family Therapy refers to the concept of 'triangles', whereby two family members form a coalition against another, and to 'family hierarchy', which refers to the need for appropriate family role-definition. In other words, as mentioned in relation to structural approaches, family members should carry out roles appropriate to their position in the family (mother or daughter or father, for example). Strategic Family Therapy also uses the concept of homework—tasks to be carried out between sessions to address problems.

Haley's (1987) Strategic Family Therapy is sometimes described as problem-solving therapy, and it shares the characteristics of other problem-solving models. These include identifying a problem that can be solved, setting goals, developing interventions to achieve the goals and examining whether or not they have been achieved. Haley's model is a short-term one, which views problems as existing in a social context and influenced by the circumstances in which families live and interact.

Collaborative Family Work has much in common with Strategic Family Therapy. Like Strategic Family Therapy, it is a short-term intervention usually delivered over six to ten weeks. Like Strategic Family Therapy, it does not seek to find the 'real' underlying problem, accepting that family problems are often maintained simply because of the way family members interact. It accepts that problems are sometimes problems because of the way families define them, and it uses the concept of re-labelling. It also uses a similar problem-solving structure to that proposed by Haley (1987), with goals and interventions to achieve goals.

Collaborative Family Work can, however, be distinguished from the work of Haley and the Strategic Family Therapists by its focus on the family as expert and the role of the professional worker as a type of coach who provides a structure in which family members solve their own problems. While Collaborative Family Work accepts that triangles and family hierarchies are often important factors in family functioning, the model is less concerned with these concepts and more interested in helping family members to develop less conflictual ways of interacting. Collaborative Family Work does not make use of the concept of paradoxical interventions, whose purpose might be difficult to understand for some family members.

Milan Systemic Model

The Milan Systemic Model was developed in Milan, Italy in the 1970s and 1980s, and has similarities to the Strategic Family Therapy model (Boscolo et al. 1987, Selvini-Palazzoli et al. 1978). It is distinguished by the mutual development of goals by the therapist and family members, and by the way it helps family members to address issues through certain techniques. The therapist tries to interrupt the 'games' that family members play—games that generally sustain problems rather than solve them. Therapists use a concept of 'positive connotation' by which family members' actions are construed in a positive way. For example, a daughter might be concerned about her mother's unwillingness to allow her independence, and upset by her mother's insistence on walking her to school each day. This can be construed in terms of the mother's concern for the daughter's safety and the daughter's natural need to develop independence.

The Milan Systemic Model includes the technique of circular questioning, which involves the therapist asking each family member to comment separately on the nature of a particular issue. They might be asked, for example, to comment on the relationship between two other members of the family. This allows family members to see what other family members think about something, and enables each family member to express their own view. It also helps family members to see that they each define problems in different ways and that the nature of problems is a matter of definition rather than absolute truth (Brown 1997; Selvini-Palazzoli et al. 1970).

Systemic therapy also uses the technique of hypothesising. This involves the family therapist—or the therapeutic team if there is more than one therapist involved—developing hypotheses about what is going on in the family and about the causes of family conflict. For example, the therapist might hypothesise that a young man argues with his sister a lot because he feels that his parents like his sister more than him and he feels isolated in the family. The family members would then be asked whether they think this is the case. This can help the family to understand the causes of the sibling conflict, and to develop strategies to address the issue of isolation rather than simply the conflict between siblings.

Another concept used in systemic therapy is that of neutrality. This involves the therapist accepting the view of family dynamics and family problems as each member presents them, even if they are very different. Therapists do not align themselves with any family member or any family member's perception of the problem. The therapist remains neutral in this respect, even though at different times they may appear to be aligned with one or another family member.

The Milan Systemic Model clearly has a lot in common with Collaborative Family Work. Both are collaborative and goal directed. Both allow family members to move at their own pace. By focusing on promoting what has worked and what has not worked in the past, Collaborative Family Work also attempts to change the interactions and game-playing that sustain negative family interactions. Collaborative Family Work uses the technique of positive connotation through its focus on reframing and relabelling negative comments and interpretations into positive ones. Like the systemic model, Collaborative Family Work focuses on individual family members' interpretations and definitions of problems. It accepts problems at face value, and as family members define them, rather than searching for the 'real' problem.

Collaborative Family Work may use the strategy of hypothesising to help family members understand blocks in communication. However, it does this cautiously. The focus of Collaborative Family Work is on the family member's definition of problems, however often the worker may feel that an alternative explanation is likely to be more useful for the family members. For example, a father may feel that it is his role to ensure that his children do not mix with young people who he believes are a poor influence on them. The worker may suggest that this view may alienate his children, who believe that they should be able to make their own decisions about their friends.

Collaborative Family Work attempts to be neutral in terms of allowing each family member to identify problems in their own terms. On the other hand, there are often occasions when workers using the Collaborative Family Work model have a statutory responsibility for a young person, and they may be working in the interests of that young person rather than, or as well as, the family as a whole. The worker may be interested in, for example, prioritising issues that relate to child protection, criminal justice or education. The general concern to promote and encourage pro-social comments and behaviours is a key component of Collaborative Family Work, and is not necessarily consistent with the concept of neutrality.

The recent family therapies

Family therapy approaches are commonly broken down into traditional approaches and more recent approaches (e.g. Goldenberg & Goldenberg 2008). Outlined below are comments in relation to cognitive behavioural family therapy, narrative therapy and solution-focused family therapy—three approaches to working with families that have been developed over recent decades.

Cognitive Behavioural Therapy

Behavioural therapy is based in learning theory (Eysenck 1959; Stuart 1980). Behavioural therapists tend to work most often with individuals, but may work with family members to help them modify the behaviour of other family members. Behaviour therapy accepts that behaviour is influenced by the consequences of actions. For example, a child may throw tantrums because each time they do so the tantrum is followed by attention from a parent. Removing the consequence (the attention) is likely to reduce the tantrums over time. The therapist can help the family to avoid rewarding or reinforcing behaviour they wish to get rid of, and to reward behaviour they would like to continue or increase. The therapist could, for example, help family members to develop an agreement whereby family members would not respond when another family member made generalisations ('You never really listen to me'), but would respond positively to reasonable requests ('I would like to talk to you for few minutes about something important to me').

Cognitive therapy, on the other hand, is based on the view that behaviour is influenced by the way people think (Ellis & Dryden 2007). The reason someone says that their partner never listens to them may simply be an interpretation or a cognitive distortion stemming from previous experiences with other partners or parents. In order to improve family relationships, family members need to be helped to understand and change the way they interpret situations.

Cognitive behavioural approaches to family therapy make use of both of these perspectives, although the many different practitioners, theorists and researchers using cognitive behavioural approaches may focus more on behavioural or more on cognitive processes. Outlined below are some of the intervention methods that are often used by cognitive behavioural therapists.

Contingency contracts involve the worker helping family members to develop agreements to exchange positive behaviours. One parent, for example, may agree to remind a young person only once about cleaning their bedroom, and in exchange the young person might agree to clean up the room within half an hour of being reminded.

Cognitive restructuring involves helping family members to restructure cognitions—in other words, review and reframe the way they think about certain things. For example, a young woman may feel that her mother is trying to control her by requiring that she come home at a certain time in the evening. The young woman could be encouraged to restructure this thought. This would involve helping her towards the view that her mother wants her home at a certain time because she cares about her safety and because when she is out late at night her mother feels that her daughter could be influenced in a negative way by the people she is with.

Cognitive behavioural therapists commonly offer a defined number of sessions, they define problems carefully and specifically, and they define what exactly family members wish to achieve. They try to understand what has preceded the unwanted behaviour and what follows, as well as how individual family members perceive the problems. The therapist can then help family members to change what occurs before problems arise, what happens after, and how family members perceive a particular event. In this way, they can address the family problems.

Collaborative Family Work has a lot in common with cognitive behavioural approaches. In fact, while for the reasons outlined earlier I have chosen not to describe this approach as therapy, Collaborative Family Work can be seen as a form of cognitive behavioural family therapy. It is concerned with identifying problems carefully, with setting goals and with analysing problems in terms of the antecedents and their consequences. It also analyses problems in terms of how they are viewed by family members, and tries to identify how cognitive distortions can impact on family functioning. It uses techniques of reframing and techniques that generally might be described as cognitive restructuring.

Collaborative Family Work varies from other cognitive behavioural approaches in its specific focus on families involved with the human services, its use of concepts such as pro-social modelling, the acceptance of the fact that goals of family work may be influenced by statutory requirements, and in its particular emphasis on working on presenting problems as the family members describe them. It also varies from some other cognitive behavioural approaches because, while workers may challenge statements and interpretations that they see as cognitive distortions, they do this cautiously and only at the client's pace. Cognitive restructuring is less of a focus compared with most cognitive behavioural approaches.

Functional Family Therapy

Reference was made in Chapter 1 to Functional Family Therapy as a successful family work method, particularly with young offenders and their families (Sexton & Alexander 2002b). Functional Family Therapy aims to integrate cognitive behavioural principles with a systems approach. It helps family members to understand why family members behave in particular ways, and tries to do this in a way that is non-blaming and does not lead to resistance from family members. Behaviour is not seen as good or bad, but as having a purpose; that is, there is something to gain or a likely consequence of the behaviour. Behaviour may be seen as an attempt to gain closeness or distance from other family members. For example, a young person may fight with a sibling not because the sibling is bad, but because this gains attention from parents. The sessions are then spent trying to understand why individual family members do certain things or why family interactions occur the way they do. Strategies can then be introduced to gain the desired consequence through another method. For example, the young man who gains a parent's attention by fighting with his sister might find another method of gaining that attention—perhaps by listening to some music together or some other activity.

Again, Collaborative Family Work shares some of the characteristics of Functional Family Therapy. While the purpose of Collaborative Family Work is not specifically to develop insight into the antecedents and consequences of particular behaviours, it does encourage detailed exploration of problems in terms of the circumstances in which they occur and why they continue. It also strongly encourages defining problems in non-blaming terms, and helping family members to develop ways of achieving their aims in more functional ways than they currently use. It is also similar to Functional Family Therapy in terms of the people it is used with. Both approaches have been used successfully with clients in the social services and juvenile justice systems.

Functional Family Therapy is different from Collaborative Family Work, however, in the way Collaborative Family Work emphasises family members as experts in their own problems, and aims to teach family members a method to deal with those problems that can be used in the future. It is also different in terms of the specific problem-solving structure offered and the focus on encouraging pro-social activities and comments.

Narrative Therapy

Narrative therapy was developed by Michael White from Adelaide in Australia and David Epston from Auckland in New Zealand (White & Epston 1989). It involves assisting people to re-examine the narratives or stories that underpin the way they have lived their lives through 're-authoring' or 're-storying' conversations. A key aim of narrative therapy is to increase people's awareness of the dominant, helpful and unhelpful stories that influence their lives.

Families and individuals often construct life stories which inhibit and control the way they live their lives. These stories generally are influenced by past experiences and social and cultural expectations. For example people will say: 'I am not good with relationships'; 'I don't trust people when they are nice to me'; 'Men are expected to be the strong ones in relationships'. Comments such as these reflect the stories people have about themselves. Their stories may be influenced by dominant discourses such as racism or patriarchy.

The aim of narrative therapy is to examine life stories and to help family members construct more productive life stories. New life stories are developed by families or individual family members for themselves with the help of the therapist. The therapist is not seen as the expert or the person who understands the 'real truth' behind a family's problems. The issue is the problem as it is described by the family members, not how it is interpreted by the therapist. The family members are the experts on their own experiences, and the therapist respects the family members' stories.

Narrative therapists use a number of techniques, including 'therapeutic letters', which may be used to summarise sessions or invite family members to sessions. They encourage family members to see problems as external to the individual or family so that the problem is seen as the problem, not the person. The family members can then work together to find ways of dealing with the problem. A problem such as child soiling might be given a name like 'Sneaky Poos', as if it is external to the child and no one is to blame for it—it is simply a problem to be dealt with by the family. In this way, the family is distanced from the problem (White & Epston 1989).

Narrative therapists also help family members identify exceptions to their problem-dominated life stories—for example, times when they had a good family relationship. This can help family members to construct different life stories. The therapists provide opportunities for family members to tell their stories to other family members or other people, and to change their stories in the process.

Collaborative Family Work draws on some of the ideas of narrative therapy. In particular, Collaborative Family Work sees the client as expert, it accepts family members' views of the problem as the problem and it sees the family members as experts in their own problems. While the practice of letter-writing is not a key feature of Collaborative Family Work, the use of carefully written notes that summarise problems, goals and strategies is central to the model. The concept of reframing family members' self-defeating comments into more productive ones is also an important part of Collaborative Family Work, as is the notion of looking for times when the problem was not there.

Perhaps the main differences between narrative therapy and Collaborative Family Work lie in the latter's focus on defining problems carefully, in an acceptance that in some cases at least it is reasonable for the workers to define behaviours as self-defeating and undesirable (child abuse, illegal drug use, school truancy, domestic violence), even if the family members do not see it that way, and in the use of the specific principles of pro-social modelling (discussed in the next chapter).

Solution-Focused Therapy

Solution-focused therapy was developed by Steve de Shazer (1988), Insoo Kim Berg (1994) and their team at the Brief Family Therapy Center in the United States. It is a goal-focused treatment developed from therapies using problem-solving and systems approaches. The key elements of solution-focused therapy include identifying a problem; identifying exceptions or times when the problem was not present; the 'miracle question', whereby the family members are asked to comment on how things would be different if they woke up one morning and the problem was not there; encouraging family members to be hopeful and see possibilities; the use of rating scales so that families can rate where they are currently in relation to a problem, where they would like to be in the future and what this would look like; and focusing on strengths.

Solution-focused therapy is centred on assisting clients to construct solutions to their problems rather than focusing on the problem itself. It is based on the assumption that the resolution of a client's presenting problem need not involve an understanding of the root cause of the problem. Solution-focused family therapy is often used in crisis intervention settings, including child protection services and school settings (Corcoran 2006).

Collaborative Family Work draws on many of the ideas of solution-focused family therapy. Both approaches focus on problem identification, goals, exceptions, scales, strengths and optimism. The key difference between solution-focused approaches and Collaborative Family Work is the latter's concern to identify and explore problems carefully, including the background to the problem and what has led to its development.

Critical and Reflective Practice

While not necessarily family work approaches, Critical and Reflective Practice have much currency in human services work and for this reason deserve a brief mention in this discussion about models and theories. Critical Practice is based on a premise that social problems are in large part socially constructed, and that client problems are often related to socio-economic or structural factors such as class and role expectations, inequality, poverty, poor housing, unemployment and inadequate social security systems. Critical theory is concerned about the oppression of groups on the basis of race, gender, age, disability, illness or poverty (Morley 2003; Spratt & Houston 1999).

Definitions of Reflective Practice vary; however, it is commonly seen as involving a process of learning and developing by examining one's own practice—it involves critical thinking and critical self-awareness. Reflective Practice recognises the value of workers' 'lived experience of practice' as a way of developing knowledge (Knott & Scagg 2010).

Collaborative Family Work has been developed as a way of working with disadvantaged, marginalised and disempowered families. It is a partnership model that aims to empower family members by giving them skills in interpersonal communication and conflict resolution. It is non-blaming, expressed in accessible language and focused on family members' own views of their world and their problems. It also aims to help family members see their problems in a social context. It is consistent with many of the values and theory of critical practice.

Reflective Practice is sometimes seen as the opposite of evidence-based practice, and I suggested in Chapter 1 that this book is rooted in the evidence-based paradigm. On the other hand, Knott and Scagg (2010) argue that Reflective Practice can exist alongside evidence-based practice, and I would argue that in many ways Collaborative Family

Work is consistent with Reflective Practice. The model has been developed using the reflective experiences of workers. I have been involved in many hundreds of debriefing sessions with workers using the model. In some cases, we have had a debriefing team including staff supervisors and managers and in other cases it has involved one-to-one debriefing or supervision. Debriefing—in other words, reflecting on what has worked and what hasn't—and thinking about what to do in the next session are fundamental to the success of the model. The debriefing (and reflection) sessions have also provided many practical examples of techniques and activities that have been used in the development of the model. Debriefing also provides an opportunity to reflect on issues of social context and disadvantage in a way that is consistent with Critical and Reflective Practice.

Chapter summary

It can be seen from this discussion that there are many models of family therapy. Some focus on differentiation from family of origin, some foster unstructured flow of emotional expression; some are concerned about boundaries and levels of enmeshment and disengagement, family triangles and hierarchies; some involve hypothesising and neutrality; some focus on antecedents and consequences and interpretations of events; some are interested in individual life stories; and some are concerned with finding solutions.

The various models have a lot in common. There is a general acceptance that past family experiences have a long-term impact on people, and that the messages from culture and family of origin are pervasive. They can lead to self-concepts and life stories that are self-defeating. Most therapies allow for the honest expression of emotion when it is appropriate. Most accept in general terms that some models of family interaction are healthier than others, and that confusion of roles in families can be destructive. Most accept that families develop repetitive patterns of interaction that can be destructive, that a focus on strengths and on reframing and relabelling can be helpful, and that changing what leads to undesired behaviour or what people gain from it can be valuable. Most agree that strategies or solutions need to be developed with families to address problems.

It can also be seen from the discussion in this chapter that Collaborative Family Work incorporates much of what is common to the various models and some of what is specific to particular models. In particular, it has a lot in common with the more recent therapies, particularly cognitive behavioural therapy. Nevertheless, it can be distinguished by its specific step-by-step structure, its strong focus on the family as expert and the worker as coach, the use of language that aims to make the model accessible, its focus on work with families in human services, and its use of the concept of pro-social modelling and reinforcement.

3
The Collaborative Family Work model

This chapter outlines the background to the Collaborative Family Work model and provides a summary of each of the steps in the model. It then discusses specific settings in which the model has been used—for example, in schools, child welfare, youth justice, outreach youth work and family support. It outlines the research support for the model, first summarising the general research relating to effective practice in human service interventions, including work with marginalised and involuntary clients, and then describing a number of specific research studies on the Collaborative Family Work model.

Background to the model

Collaborative Family Work has its origins in problem-solving models that have been used by workers in the human services for many years. They have been utilised effectively by social workers, psychologists, family support workers and family therapists with clients in a wide array of settings, including child welfare, youth justice, mental health, drug treatment, school welfare and hospitals.

Perhaps the first person to popularise problem-solving in social work was Helen Harris Perlman (1957) in her book *Social Casework: A Problem-solving Process*. William Reid and Laura Epstein published *Task-centred Casework* in 1972, which again outlined a problem-solving model for casework practice. This book became one of the best-selling texts in the human services, and was translated into multiple languages. It was the precursor to many more books and articles on the task-centred model of practice, including *Family Problem-solving* (Reid 1985). In a recent book dedicated to the memory of William Reid, Videka and Blackburn (2010: 183) comment that: 'Reid's work on time limits in treatment, the task-centred practice model and the role of science in knowledge development for social work transformed the profession.'

Reid's work was based on an acceptance that there were growing numbers of people in need of assistance and increasing demands on resources, and in many cases short-term interventions of six to twelve weeks were the most that clients in the welfare system could be offered. He emphasised that gains could be made by focusing on clients' problems in the 'here and now', by focusing on problems as the client described them, by accepting the client's problems at face value rather than reinterpreting them according to the worker's assessment, and by supporting the client's own problem-solving actions. William Reid continued writing until his death in 2003, and his work incorporated many of the more recent ideas and models for work in the human services—it was evidence based, strengths based, focused on finding solutions and focused on helping people to solve their own problems. Reid's task-centred model also made use of the techniques of cognitive behavioural therapy (Reid 2000).

Collaborative Family Work also draws on another body of theoretical and empirical work—that of Don Andrews and his colleagues, psychologists who work in the criminal justice field. Some of their early work focused on the application of learning theory to the supervision of offenders (Andrews et al. 1979) and analysed the use of pro-social modelling by probation officers. It is clear from their work, as well as more recent work (e.g. Cherry 2005)—including my own research (Trotter 1990, 1996, 2004, 2006)—that when human service workers model pro-social behaviours and encourage and reinforce pro-social comments and actions in their clients, those clients have better outcomes—including reduced levels of offending and child abuse.

The model also draws on early work on client socialisation by Ronald Rooney (1992), and James Jones and Abraham Alcabes (1993), which suggests that clients of justice, child protection and drug-treatment agencies—clients who are in many cases involuntary—need to be engaged in a helping relationship with their workers in order to achieve good outcomes. However, this helping relationship may be compromised by the authority that workers must exercise and the difficulty clients have in understanding the dual role of the worker as both helper and authority figure. Jones and Alcabes (1993) refer to client socialisation as 'the Achilles heel of the helping professions'. They argue that the client only becomes a client when they accept that the worker is someone who can genuinely help with their problems, even though the worker has authority over them.

The model also draws heavily on the 'what works' literature. The general principles of effective practice are summarised in my earlier book, *Working with Involuntary Clients* (Trotter 2006) as follows: services are accessible at times when they are needed; the aims of the service agency and those of the worker are understood by the client; the clients have a good understanding of the role of the worker and what is expected of them; the worker models and reinforces pro-social values and actions, and makes appropriate use of challenging or confrontation; the worker works with client definitions of problems; the worker helps the client to develop skills, (including social skills), which can help with their (the client's) goals; the focus is on practical issues rather than feelings or insight; the worker takes a holistic approach to client issues rather than focus only on particular problems or symptoms; the worker encourages the client to focus on problems that are related to their anti-social or self destructive behaviours (e.g. illegal drug use, child abuse, offending, truancy, anger); and the worker presents an optimistic view to clients about their potential for change.

Another principle of effective practice referred to in *Working with Involuntary Clients* and in other texts (e.g. Andrews & Bonta 2010; Taxman & Bouffard 2002) is sometimes described as 'therapeutic integrity'. In other words, are the services or programs delivered in a way that is consistent with the way in which they are supposed to be delivered? There is evidence that professional human service workers often vary their interventions according to their own orientation or interests, and that the effectiveness of their interventions is closely related to the extent to which they are delivered as they were intended. The literature provides many examples of services that in practice bear little resemblance to the theory or practice principles on which they were developed (Dowden & Andrews 2003; Sexton & Turner 2010; Trotter 2004).

The Collaborative Family Work model draws particularly on three key principles: problem-solving and its focus on working with client definitions of problems towards client goals; pro-social modelling, which accept that workers influence their clients towards particular behaviours through a process of modelling and reinforcement; and role clarification, including the need for the client to accept that the worker is someone who can help them with their problems. My earlier book, *Working with Involuntary Clients* (Trotter 2006) provides more detail on these approaches.

The Collaborative Family Work model has been influenced by a number of authors who have applied problem-solving models to work with families. Epstein and Bishop developed a family problem-solving model in 1981, outlined in Problem centred systems and the family (Gurman & Kniskern 1981). Gerald Patterson and Marion Forgatch (1987, 1989) published a two-volume book, *Parents and Adolescents Living Together*, with the second volume focused on family problem-solving with a particular focus on brainstorming and evaluating solutions.

William Reid developed his task-centred model for working with families in a book titled *Family Problem-Solving* in 1985. Reid divides the model into three stages. The first includes problem survey, initial problem exploration and formulation, formulating problems, determining target problems and goals, orientation and contract, detailed exploration of the target problems, initial session task, post-task discussion and planning initial home task. The middle phase includes task and problem reviews, problem focusing, contextual analysis, session tasks, and home and environmental tasks. The third and last stage includes differential use of interventions and the final interview.

More recent work on family problem-solving has been undertaken by Wade et al. (2006) and Ahmadi et al. (2010). Wade and colleagues report on a study where young people (aged 5 to 16 years) were recovering from traumatic brain injury. Families, including children, were offered seven bi-weekly core group sessions followed by four individualised sessions using the problem-solving model. They used the acronym ABCDE—Aim, Brainstorm, Choose, Do it, Evaluate—to describe the steps in the model. Sessions focused on general goals as well as goals relating directly to the brain injury, based on the evidence that brain injury impacts on multiple issues for family members.

Ahmadi et al. (2010) report on work undertaken in Tehran using a family problem-solving model with married couples, based on the following steps: introduction to the model; prioritising issues and increasing optimism; creating solutions; evaluating solutions; solving problems; and evaluation.

There is therefore a long history of human service interventions based on problem-solving principles. The Collaborative Family Work model has much in common with these models, but has been developed further through ongoing use and evaluation of the model in welfare and youth justice settings. It also draws on principles of pro-social modelling and role clarification, as discussed in this and later chapters.

We now move on to a description of the Collaborative Family Work model, beginning with a discussion about preparation of families, working in family homes, working in pairs, pro-social modelling and rating scales. This is followed by a summary of the steps in the model. More detail is provided on each of the steps in subsequent chapters.

The Collaborative Family Work model

Preparation

Prior to beginning work with the family group (any two family members), the worker discusses with the family members the nature of the family work and the role of both the workers and the family members in the process. These discussions can then be followed up in the first session. Preparing the family members for the sessions can be important in gaining the cooperation of the family from the outset.

Home-based model

Family counselling sessions may be held in the worker's office or in the family's home. Home-based sessions have advantages, and the students and professionals who participated in my research studies (Trotter 2002, 2010) have undertaken most of their sessions in the family home. Certainly, family members are more likely to participate when this occurs.

Co-counselling

It is common, when using this model, for two workers to work with the family. The evaluations referred to later in this chapter for the most part involved two workers offering the family work. The aim in using two workers or co-counsellors is both educational and supportive. It also addresses some of the safety issues related to home visiting.

Generally, when working with two workers, it is common for the workers to alternate roles. One worker leads the discussion on a particular issue free from interruptions from the other worker. At the completion of the segment of work—perhaps for ten minutes or so—the second worker who has been taking notes summarises the content of the discussion with a particular focus on reflecting the views of each participant. This may be done with the assistance of a notepad or large piece of paper placed on the wall in the room in which the work is taking place.

As the workers become more comfortable with each other, they may vary this method and develop less formal ways of working together. Nevertheless, it is important that workers talk to each other about how they will work together before the family work begins.

There are some advantages in working with two workers. Workers may feel more confident having someone working alongside them, and they may be more comfortable working in clients' homes if there are two workers. The presence of two workers provides an opportunity for the workers to learn from each other and to improve their skills by giving feedback to each other about how they conduct the sessions. Similarly, two workers can plan together and debrief together.

Having two workers may allow for continuity of contact between a primary worker and a client family. Sometimes a worker may feel that their client—for example, a young person on a probation order—would benefit from family work; however, the worker does not feel sufficiently confident or skilled to undertake a series of family work sessions with the family. In this situation, the worker might involve a second worker who has confidence and expertise in working with families. By involving a second person in the family work, the primary worker can offer the family work as a separate but complementary process to the ongoing work they are doing with the young person. The worker may then continue to see the young person on an individual basis between family work sessions. This allows for continuity of supervision for the young person, and it takes advantage of both the credibility the primary worker has with the young person and their family, and the knowledge the worker may have about the young person and the family. It allows the primary worker to follow up issues that have arisen in the family sessions, and to reinforce the work that has been done when the family work intervention has been completed. The worker can work to maintain the gains that may have been produced in the family work sessions.

Two workers can model the behaviour they are seeking from clients. The workers may disagree, for example, on some aspect of the intervention. In fact, there are many times in work with families where individual judgements need to be made about what to do next. One worker may think that more time needs to be spent on exploring a problem, whereas the other worker may feel that they are getting bogged down in the problem exploration and need to move on to identifying goals. On these occasions, two workers have an opportunity to show the family members how to successfully negotiate a disagreement. The two workers can model a respectful and collaborative negotiation in front of the family, which then reaches a compromise agreement.

Sometimes the presence of two workers can provide an opportunity for one of the workers to support less powerful family members. For example, in situations where one member of the family may feel intimidated, or is particularly inarticulate, or has an intellectual or learning disability, or is a reluctant participant in family work, it may be appropriate for one worker to take a particular role in helping the client to feel comfortable and ensuring that the experience is a positive one for that family member.

There are, of course, also disadvantages to working in

pairs. Sometimes these are related to inevitable differences human beings have when they work together. One worker may feel that the other is not contributing enough to the conversation. The other may feel that their partner is too dominant. One worker may feel that family members are warming to the other worker and not to them. The model should provide the means by which workers can deal with issues such as these; nevertheless, it must be acknowledged that using two workers adds another dimension to the work and another challenge for workers.

The worker–worker relationship is likely be enhanced if each worker applies the skills outlined in the model to working with their co-worker. It is the responsibility of the worker to be understanding, positive, strengths-based and goal-oriented with their fellow worker in the same way they are with their clients. Failure to get on with the co-worker is a poor outcome in the same way that failure to get on with the family members is a poor outcome.

Pro-social modelling

Pro-social modelling and reinforcement constitute an intervention technique based in behavioural theory (referred to in Chapter 2). Practitioners in the human services influence their clients through modelling and reinforcing particular cognitions, emotions and behaviours of their clients. A number of studies have found that workers who model pro-social values and who reinforce pro-social values have clients with better outcomes than workers who do not do so. This has been shown in criminal justice settings (Andrews & Bonta 2003; Dowden & Andrews 2004), in child protection settings (Trotter 2004; Gough 1993) and in drug treatment settings (Barber 1995). It is on this basis that training in pro-social modelling and reinforcement has been widely offered in probation and youth justice services in the United Kingdom and elsewhere. Pro-social modelling is described as a well-known model of intervention in the US Justice Department publication *Implementing Evidence-Based Policy and Practice in Community Corrections* (Guevara & Solomon 2009).

There is some evidence that the extent of the influence of modelling and reinforcement depends on the quality of the relationship between the worker and the client. Andrews et al. (1979) undertook a study that remains relevant today because it has not been replicated. They examined tape recordings of interviews between Canadian probation officers and their clients, and found that probation officers who modelled and reinforced pro-social values and who also made use of reflective listening practices had clients with lower recidivism rates compared with the recidivism rates of the clients of other probation officers. In other words, modelling and reinforcement were more influential when workers had good relationships and related caring skills. On a similar theme, a study by Rex and Maltravers (1998) in a corrections setting in the United Kingdom suggested that modelling was more influential if clients perceived their workers to be legitimate—in other words, if the worker had a moral authority in the mind of the client.

The importance of relationship factors in human services work has been acknowledged in the literature for more than 50 years (e.g. Perlman 1957) and continues today (Compton, Galaway & Cournoyer 2005; Hepworth et al. 2006). One aspect of the relationship is the 'use of self'. While the meaning of the term is somewhat ambiguous, Dewane (2006) defines 'self' as including personality, belief system, relational dynamics and self-disclosure. The argument presented in this book and elsewhere (Trotter & Ward 2012) is that the pro-social orientation of the worker and the practices of pro-social modelling and reinforcement can be seen as an important aspect of the use of self and of the worker–client relationship.

The practice of pro-social modelling and reinforcement

Modelling may be pro-social or supportive of social conventions, such as obeying the law; it may be pro-criminal or supportive of criminal or anti-social values and activities; or it may fall somewhere between these two extremes. Pro-social modelling and reinforcement refer to the way in which those who work with involuntary clients model and reinforce pro-social values and behaviours in their interactions with clients. The following are examples from the limited research on pro-social modelling conducted by Andrews et al. (1979) in a criminal justice setting, in criminal justice and child protection (Trotter 2006) and discussed in Cherry (2005).

Pro-social modelling involves the worker being honest and reliable; following up on tasks; respecting other people's feelings, expressing views about the value of pro-social pursuits, such a non-criminal friends, good family relations, work or attending school; acknowledging the client's own perspective; and demonstrating concern for the client's welfare when appropriate. It entails interpreting people's motives positively, and also being optimistic about the rewards that can be obtained by living within the law.

The following example illustrates the potential influence of pro-social modelling (Trotter 2002, 2004). In a study undertaken with child protection, 280 clients were asked to comment on the extent to which their workers were punctual, did the things that they said they would do and responded to phone calls. The clients' responses were then correlated with outcome measures, which included client satisfaction with the service provided, worker ratings of client progress and the length of time clients remained under the supervision of child protection. Each of the worker practices was related at statistically significant levels to each of the outcome measures. In other words, when the workers modelled basic values of respect and reliability, the outcomes for their clients were better. When they did not model these practices, the outcomes for their clients were worse. Significantly, the workers themselves were generally unaware of the potential impact of these practices.

It is evident from the Canadian study (Andrews et al. 1979) and two Australian studies (Trotter 1996, 2004) referred to earlier that more pro-social workers are inclined not only to model pro-social comments and actions for their clients, but also to reinforce their clients' pro-social comments and actions. Some examples of client pro-social actions and comments include those related to compliance with a court order such as keeping appointments, not offending and following special conditions such as attending for drug treatment. Other client pro-social actions include working through problem-solving processes, accepting responsibility for offences, empathy for others and the use of non-physical means of discipline of children. Pro-social workers tend to reinforce comments and actions that value non-criminal activities and associations, including family, sport, non-criminal friends, hobbies and attending school or work. Pro-social workers are also likely to reinforce expressions that are fair, non-sexist and non-racist. They reinforce optimistic attitudes—for example, expressing a belief that life without crime is achievable, that goals can be achieved, that workers can help and that clients can change.

Workers reinforce these things primarily through their body language—for example, smiling, attentive listening, leaning forward—and the use of praise. Positive reinforcement can also be provided by, for example, the worker giving time to the client; attending court with the client and providing positive evidence; reducing the frequency of contact (if the client sees this as positive); helping the client to find a job or accommodation; making home visits or meeting a client outside the office; writing a positive report; advocating for the client with other agencies/professionals, such as social security or the police; and making positive comments in file notes.

The concepts of pro-social modelling and reinforcement are grounded in learning theory. They involve clients copying or imitating behaviour and linking subsequent pro-social behaviour with positive rewards. For example, the fact that a client has kept appointments, attended job interviews and not reoffended can lead to reductions in the frequency of visits, positive progress reports and praise from the supervisor. A learning pattern may be established, which leads the client towards more pro-social values and behaviours. While the concepts are based in learning theory, they are nevertheless consistent with the growing voice for strengths-based and relationship-oriented interventions in the human services (e.g. Howe 2010; Maruna & LeBel 2010). The process of modelling and reinforcement may also include challenging or confrontation in certain contexts. This involves the worker identifying and responding to clients' rationalisations, or procriminal comments and activities. There is some evidence that the technique of challenging clients can be effective in improving client outcomes if it is used sparingly and within the context of a positive relationship (Trotter 2004; Hepworth et al. 2006). From an ethical standpoint, confrontation needs to be implemented in a way that takes a person's strengths and weaknesses into account, and in this sense ought to exhibit care. For a detailed discussion about ethical issues involved in pro-social modelling, see Trotter and Ward (2012).

As mentioned earlier, there is evidence that pro-social modelling and reinforcement lead to improved client outcomes. On the other hand, research indicates that pro-criminal modelling leads to poorer outcomes for clients (Andrews & Bonta 2003; Trotter 2002, 2004, 2006; Dowden et al. 2004). Pro-criminal modelling involves the opposite of pro-social modelling—strengthening (dis)values such as dishonesty, disrespect, callousness and unreliability, and excusing inappropriate behaviours that have led the client into the system (criminal activity or child abuse, for example).

Pro-social modelling is therefore one of the core practices that relate to positive outcomes in work in the human services, and the use of pro-social modelling skills is an integral part of the Collaborative Family Work model.

Rating scales

The model makes use of family functioning rating scales and problem rating scales. The value of these scales has been highlighted in research by Fischer (2004) and Miller et al. (2006), which found that the client's perceived improvement between sessions was an important predictor for adherence and treatment outcome. It also found that clients' retention rates increased significantly if they had the opportunity to voice their perception of progress between sessions on a regular basis and in a systematic way.

Rating scales are completed in each session by the family members in order to give a sense of the extent to which the family members are progressing in relation to general family functioning and in relation to specific problems that have been identified. Figures 3.1 and 3.2 show the rating scales developed for use with Collaborative Family Work.

Figure 3.1: General family functioning rating scale

To be completed by worker or family member at each session for each family member.

Circle a number on the scale 1 to 5 that corresponds with how you feel about the family.

1	2	3	4	5

Family relationships in our family at the present time are:
1. Poor—there is continual arguing, people rarely speak to each other, there is virtually no communication other than to dispute things.
2. Unsatisfactory—there is some positive communication between at least some of the family members; however, overall family relationships are problematic and/or unsatisfying.
3. Satisfactory—family members communicate on some issues and there is some satisfaction in family life, although things could be a lot better.
4. Very satisfactory—basically things are okay within the family, and family members generally communicate without too many problems. However, things could still be better.
5. Good—family life is not characterised by arguments or poor communication, and family members find it generally satisfying.

Date _____ Session No. _____
Person (e.g. mother, young person) _____

Figure 3.2: Rating scale for family problems

To be completed by the workers or family members at each session for each problem that is being worked on.

One rating scale should be completed by each family member.

Circle a number on the scale 1 to 5 that corresponds with how you feel about the problem.

1	2	3	4	5

1. Poor—the problem is very serious and makes it very difficult to cope with everyday life.
2. Unsatisfactory—the problem is very serious but you are able to cope with most everyday tasks.
3. Satisfactory—the problem is serious but does not interfere with your everyday life.
4. Very satisfactory—the problem is not that serious and you are able to cope with it reasonably well.
5. Good—there is no real problem.

Date _____ Session No. _____

Problem _____

Person (e.g. mother, young person) _____

The family functioning scale is introduced and completed by each family member early in the first session so that the workers have a baseline against which they can compare the progress of the family as the intervention progresses. Problem scales are introduced following or during problem exploration, to provide a baseline for future comparison and to help define the problem.

Mapping the scales over the weeks of the family work can show workers and clients that progress is being made from week to week, and can show family members how they have progressed during the period of the intervention.

Figure 3.3 shows the plotting of the family functioning scale of a family as assessed by the primary client over eight sessions of family work. This chart can be shown to family members each week to show their progress. Alternatively, if the scales are not moving in an upward direction, then this can be discussed with family members and they can be asked why they are not progressing and what can be done differently in order to progress. It may also be that different family members have different ratings; again, where this is the case, some discussion about why family members feel differently can take place.

Figure 3.3: Family functioning over eight weeks

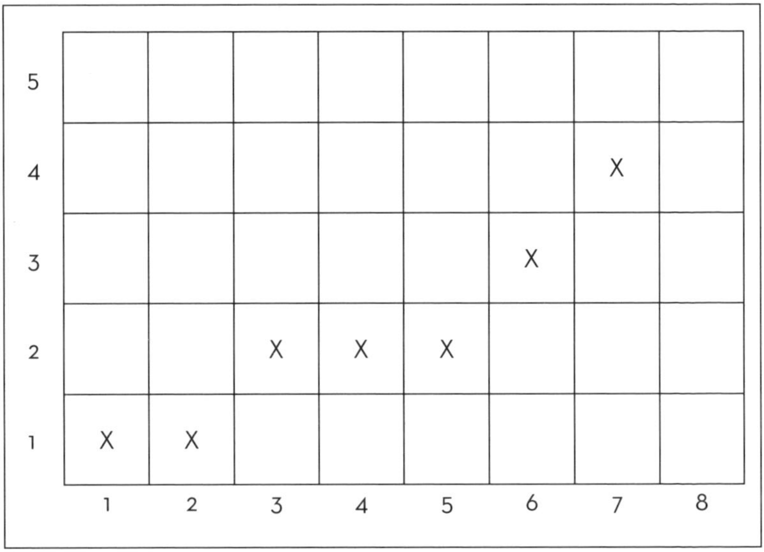

While it is desirable for the ratings to increase or at least remain the same at each session, there may be occasions when the scales move downwards for some family members but this still reflects progress. For example, a family member may feel that everything is fine in the family; however, when issues are raised by other family members, they may realise that there are problems of which they were unaware, or about which they were in denial. Sometimes one family member may cause problems for others without realising they are doing it.

In addition to helping to define the level of family functioning and the seriousness of problems, rating scales can also help to define goals. Family members will often have goals that are hard to define. For example, a goal might be to improve communication in the family. The worker might ask the family members to rate on a scale of 1 to 5 the current level of communication using the problem rating scale in Figure 3.2. The workers might then ask the family members to say why they have rated it at this level. They can explore the specific factors that have influenced the rating of the family members—for example, frequent arguments, an absence of respectful conversation, abusive comments and swearing at each other.

The workers can then ask the family members to identify where they would like to be on the rating scale in, say, four weeks after working on the issue in the family work sessions. Their goal may be to increase the rating from, say, 2 to 4. The family members can then discuss what would be different and how the family would interact if family communication were rated 4. This can help family members to develop a picture of what is possible, and allows the workers to help the family members examine their progress after the specified period.

One other advantage of using rating scales is that each family member can make their own decisions about the rating, and it provides an opportunity for each family member to have a say.

Supervision and debriefing

Reference was made earlier to the importance of debriefing and supervision for workers. I suggested that this has elements of reflective practice in the process. The debriefing usually occurs one or two days after each session with the family. It involves the worker or workers presenting what they have done in the session, which steps of the model they have covered, how the family responded to the various discussions and activities, and what they plan to do in the next session.

The debriefing often involves helping the workers to stay on track. In other words, helping them to identify how what they did in the last session relates to the steps in the model. For example, the workers may have discussed a particular problem in some depth, but may not have worked through the process of deciding whether this problem was the most appropriate one to work on at that time. Or the workers may have helped the family members to develop a particular strategy but did not do this in relation to a specific goal.

Sometimes the debriefing focuses on the workers' feelings about the work. This might involve, for example, their concern that the family is not progressing as they had hoped, or that one family member was uncooperative and angry, and they found this difficult to deal with.

It might also provide an opportunity to discuss issues of disadvantage consistent with the critical practice perspective referred to in Chapter 2. Those in the debrief team might reflect on the difficulties faced by Indigenous families, for example, and might discuss how they can ensure that the family work is sensitive to the cultural norms and expectations of the family.

The debriefing involves similar principles to working with the families—non-blaming, supportive and strengths focused. Ideally, the debriefing will be part of the regular supervision offered to professional staff. Regular debriefing is an important part of the model and if it is not available then co-workers might arrange specific debriefing sessions between themselves where they go through what they did in the previous session, why they did this, what alternatives there might have been and what they plan to do in the next session. If they are working alone, without support, then it is important that workers take the time to personally reflect on these things, both themselves and with the family.

The model

The Collaborative Family Work model is summarised here. The following chapters address the steps in the model in detail; however, this section aims to give the reader an over-view before examining the model in depth.

Ground rules and role clarification

Initially, the worker reviews with family members what is involved in the sessions, including the way they will be con-ducted and how the model works. Copies of the steps in the model can be taken by the worker to the family home if the sessions take place there, or displayed in the worker's office.

The aim here is to generate discussion about how the sessions will be conducted. Some of the issues that should be discussed include those relating to confidentiality: Who will know about what goes on in the sessions? Will the informa-tion be discussed with others? What if disclosures are made about child abuse or further offences? Can information from the sessions be included in court reports? Other issues include: can individual family members have discussions with the counsellor between sessions, and will these discussions be confidential? Is the counsellor neutral or acting on behalf of a young person who is the primary client? Will the worker undertake follow-up tasks between sessions—for example, speaking to school teachers. Will the sessions be held in the family home or in the office, or at some other venue? Is participation voluntary? Is the TV to be turned off? Can anyone leave at any time? What happens if one family member is abusive towards another, or if people try to talk over each other?

The worker then writes down the guidelines for conducting the sessions so that all family members can see them. This results in a number of written guidelines or ground rules—for example, sessions will be for 45 minutes once a week; abusive language will not be accepted; the TV and phones will be turned off; family members may leave the session temporarily if they are feeling distressed; the content of sessions will not be discussed with anyone outside of the sessions; all family members will be invited to all sessions.

Identify issues you would like to change (problem survey)

Each family member is then asked to describe issues that are of concern to them, or things that they would like to change. The workers prompt family members so that a full picture of the issues is presented (How are things at school? Who are your friends? Do you have enough money?). The worker then lists the problems of each family member on a whiteboard or piece of paper.

The workers also encourage family members to express problems in non-blaming terms. For example, the worker might reframe problems for the client. A 12-year-old boy might say that his biggest problem is his sister: 'She goes out whenever she likes and teases me all the time.' This might be reframed as: 'It upsets me that my mother does not have fair rules about what my sister is allowed to do and what I am allowed to do. I feel like they are ganging up on me.'

The workers then try to identify common family problems. For example, concern about different expectations for family members might be a common issue. Failure to listen to each other might be another common concern.

Decide what to work on first (problem ranking)

The next stage of the process involves attempting to reach agreement with the family members as to which problems are to be worked on in the short and longer term.

In making a decision about which problems to address, the following factors should be taken into account:

- It is vital that the problem or problems to be worked on are the clients' problems.

- All or most family members should agree that they are important.

- If family members have different problems, it may be necessary to work on one problem for each family member involved.

- Problems with achievable solutions should be addressed first. It might be best, for example, to start with a problem concerning pocket money rather than a problem with a parent who is not involved in the counselling and has no interest in the family.

- It is better to deal with problems where there are resources available to help—for example, if the family has a problem with lack of adequate housing, then it is much easier to deal with this if there is a possibility of getting better housing.

- If one family member is subject to a formal mandate or authority, it may be appropriate to start with formal requirements—for example, if a child is to be expelled from school unless certain things occur, or if a young person is required to undertake certain actions as part of a court order, then this should take precedence.

- If the family or any family members are facing an immediate crisis, this of course may need to be dealt with immediately. For instance, if the family is homeless, this might have to take immediate priority.

- The model focuses on practical issues. The focus should be on issues such as communication, relationships, housing, employment or finances, rather than intra-psychic issues such as self-esteem, anxiety or depression.

Goals: What do we want to achieve?

The next step involves setting clear and specific goals, which are agreed on by the worker and the clients and are directly related to the problem or problems to be addressed. For example:

For Amy and Mrs L to reach agreement on whether Amy should continue to see her boyfriend and if so how often and where she should see him. This goal to be achieved by Week 7.

Some other examples of goals that have been set by workers who have used the model include the goal of developing communication between a father and son when all communication had ceased, coming to an agreement between a mother and daughter regarding the amount of freedom the young person should be allowed and reuniting a young woman living away from home with her family.

Explore the issue in more detail
The next stage involves a detailed exploration of the problem with the family in order to get a clear picture of the nature and degree of the problem and to ascertain what has been done previously to address it. It is important that this is done thoroughly so that realistic strategies to address the problem can be developed. Questions the family members should address include:

- What is the history of the problem?
- When does it occur?
- How did it begin?
- What has the family done previously to address the problem?
- Have these things helped or hindered?
- What is the client getting out of it?
- Are there occasions when the problem is not present?

Strategies/tasks: Work out ways of achieving the goals
Strategies or tasks (terms that are used interchangeably in this book) are then developed by the worker and family members to address the goals. Strategies may be carried out in the family work sessions—for example, role-play, teaching listening skills, helping family members acknowledge what

other family members are saying, brainstorming solutions or expressing problems in a non-blaming way. Strategies may be carried out at home—for example, engaging in mutually enjoyable activities, spending specified time together, a mother visiting a school or a child coming home early in return for the mother providing more pocket money. The worker might also have strategies or tasks—for example, approaching social security.

Review how we are going

As the family work progresses, it is important to regularly revise what has been done and where the family is in relation to the steps in the model. This involves the use of written summaries of ground rules, problems, goals and strategies. In the final session, a review of what has been achieved can be undertaken and strategies put in place to maintain any gains that have been made.

RIDGES

As discussed earlier in one of the agencies where this model has been used, the workers use the acronym 'RIDGES' to help staff members remember the steps in the model (see Figure 1.1).

The use of acronyms such as RIDGES can help workers using the model to readily recall the steps, and can be particularly useful for those who don't use the model frequently. The RIDGES steps are commonly taken by workers to the family home and displayed on the wall of the room in which the sessions are undertaken.

Flexibility of the model

I referred earlier to the concept of therapeutic integrity—in other words, delivering services in the way they were intended to be delivered. As mentioned, research suggests that if workers do not deliver services as intended, then they are unlikely to gain the expected outcomes (Sexton & Turner 2010; Dowden et al. 2003; Trotter 2004). This applies to the Collaborative Family Work model. I cannot stress enough that workers must work through each section of the model. If family members are not prepared and don't know what they are getting into, they are more likely to drop out. There is little to be gained by beginning work on one issue when there may be other, more important, issues that have not been explored. There is no point in setting goals if you don't really know what the problem is, and there is no point in setting tasks and strategies if you don't know what you are aiming to achieve. It is my experience with the Collaborative Family Work interventions that I have been involved in that when family members discontinue the family work, it is because their workers have deviated from the model and become lost in the process.

It is important that workers follow the model. At the same time, though, there is a need to approach the work with a degree of flexibility. This does not mean setting tasks to address a problem before the issue has been explored or before goals have been developed, or dispensing with family preparation. However, it does mean that if workers are in the process of developing tasks in relation to one issue and another important issue arises, then it may be appropriate to return to the problem survey stage of the model. It is fundamental that the workers and the family members know where they are in relation to the model at any given time, and that they follow through with the steps in the model. At the same time, they need to be flexible and there will be times when they move around within the stages of the model.

Sometimes people ask whether the steps in the model should be carried out over six consecutive weeks, with each week devoted to each step. Usually the first meeting is devoted to clarifying roles and developing ground rules and the second meeting will usually be concerned with identifying issues for family members. It is usually not until the third or fourth meeting that workers and clients begin to develop tasks to address the family members' goals and problems. The model should be used flexibly, however. For example, the model allows for facilitative strategies that don't relate to specific goals but may be used because the workers feel they want to give the family members some concrete things to do. These tasks may occur in the session or at home, and might involve, for example, commenting on what family members like about each other or writing up ground rules.

It may also be that workers use this model for shorter periods. It can be used over one or two sessions rather than the six to ten sessions I have recommended. This simply involves working through the model more quickly, and of necessity in a more superficial way. Nevertheless, short-term problem-solving with families can be successful in the same way that brief therapies can be successful (Kim 2006).

Evidence in support of problem-solving

In discussing the background to Collaborative Family Work, I pointed out that it has its origins in empirical work relating to role clarification, pro-social modelling and problem-solving, and it has been developed based on 'what works' principles. In other words, the model has been developed using evidence-based principles and practices. Reference was made earlier in the chapter to the research support for these principles, and the literature is reviewed in my earlier book *Working with Involuntary Clients* (Trotter 2006).

Many human services texts argue for a focus on strengths (Compton, Galaway & Cournoyer 2005; Harms 2007; O'Hara & Weber 2006), and there has been criticism of problem-solving models as being too negative. Locke, Garrison and Winship (1998), for example, suggest that a focus on problems can invite defensiveness and resistance, and that focusing on problems or what is wrong is unproductive. They argue that a focus on problems negates a strengths focus. On the other hand, there have been many studies conducted over many years that have pointed to the importance of defining problems carefully and in some detail before moving to solve problems (see Trotter 1999 for a summary).

This is not to argue that strengths-based work is not important. On the contrary, my research with involuntary clients continually points to the importance of non-blaming, rewarding and strengths-based work (Trotter 2004, 2006, 2010). Focusing on strengths—particularly those of a pro-social nature—is a core component of Collaborative Family Work. However, every problem and every solution is different, and until the clients and the workers understand the nature of the problems from the clients' perspective, it is generally not helpful to try to seek a solution.

No doubt the most persuasive argument in favour of problem-solving models is that they work. Problem-solving models and interventions—sometimes referred to as problem-solving therapy—include similar steps: identify the problems; decide which problem or problems to work on; set goals; develop solutions; and review. As discussed earlier, these approaches have been shown to be effective in a wide range of situations with both individuals and groups. They have been shown to work with depressed older adults in methadone maintenance treatment (Rosen, Morse & Reynolds 2011) where those undertaking the study have argued that problem-solving therapy (PST) is particularly suitable for this group, as it is less cognitively demanding than other therapies. Problem-solving therapy has also been shown to be effective in reducing suicidal behaviour and depression in a study with young people in Sri Lanka (Perera & Kathriarachchi 2011). A meta-analysis of thirteen randomised studies of the use of problem-solving therapy for depression concludes that there is no doubt that PST can be an effective treatment for depression, although it also suggests that more research is needed to determine when and in what circumstances it is most effective (Cuijpers, van Straten & Warmerda 2007).

A meta-analysis of 31 studies of problem-solving therapy by Malouff, Thorsteinsson and Shutte (2007) refers to the steps in PST as: (1) identify a problem; (2) define a problem; (3) understand the problem; (4) set goals; (5) generate solutions; (6) choose the best alternatives; (7) implement the chosen alternatives; and (8) evaluate the efficacy. The study found that PST was 'significantly more effective than no treatment, treatment as usual and placebo' (2007: 1). It established that PST was effective with both groups and individuals, and that it was most effective when there was an orientation to problem-solving offered to clients, where homework was assigned and where a developer of PST helped to conduct the study.

Further support for problem-solving in work in the human services is seen in the studies of cognitive behavioural programs directed at both groups and individuals. As discussed earlier, cognitive behavioural interventions commonly include a problem-solving component along with strategies to address distorted and unproductive thinking. In recent years, they have proved effective in work in criminal justice, child protection, mental health and treatment for addictions (Barber 2002; Corcoran 2002; Kolko 2002; Polki, Ervast & Huupponen 2004; Wilson & Horner 2005).

Three studies undertaken in criminal justice settings in Australia, Canada and the United States illustrate the value of problem-solving when accompanied by the other evidence-based practice skills (Trotter 1996; Bourgeon et al. 2010; Robinson et al. 2011). The researchers from the different studies collaborated with each other, and each of the studies built on the earlier studies. In each of the studies, training was provided for supervisors of offenders—for example, probation and parole officers—in effective supervision skills, including problem-solving, role clarification and pro-social modelling. The supervisors were also trained in the use of cognitive behavioural therapy techniques, particularly in the Bourgeon and Robinson studies. Each of the studies found that the workers made more use of the techniques after training, and the offenders under their supervision reoffended significantly less often compared with control groups where supervising workers had not received similar training.

It is fair to say that there is now a persuasive body of evidence that the problem-solving practices at the core of Collaborative Family Work are effective in work with clients in the welfare and criminal justice systems. But do these principles apply to work with family groups? There is evidence that family problem-solving models also lead to good outcomes for clients.

I referred earlier to a study by Ahmadi et al. (2010), which found increased levels of marital satisfaction following around fifteen sessions of family problem-solving with maladjusted couples in Tehran, compared with a matched control group with no treatment. Reference was also made to a study by Wade et al. (2006), which found positive results for the use of short-term family problem-solving with families with a young person (aged 5 to 16 years) recovering from brain injury, using a five-step problem-solving model—Aim, Brainstorm, Choose, Do it, Evaluate (ABCDE). In another study, a twelve-session family problem-solving intervention was offered to families recruited from a Head Start program in Canada (Drummond et al. 2005). The workers used a model based on three steps: (1) evaluate options; (2) can anyone help?; (3) agree and notice the difference. They found improvements in parent–child interactions compared with a non-treatment control group.

It is clear that problem-solving can be effective. The argument that problem-solving methods are too negative can be countered by the evidence in support of their effectiveness. Nevertheless, it is important that problem-solving is accompanied by a focus on strengths—an important component of Collaborative Family Work.

Evaluations of the Collaborative Family Work model

Collaborative Family Work, the model for family intervention presented in this book, has been used in numerous settings over the past 20 years. During this period, it has progressively been evaluated and modified based on the feedback from both family members who participated in the sessions and the staff members involved. The real-life (but de-identified) case studies presented in this book are taken from the work done by these workers.

In most cases, when workers have used the model with

families, formal evaluations have not been conducted. In some cases, however, formal client and worker evaluations of the model have been conducted. Outlined below are the situations in which these evaluations have taken place. This is followed by an outline of the responses to the evaluation by participating family members and workers.

During the 1990s, a series of family work classes were offered to final-year social work students (Trotter 2000). Each of the students undertook twelve classes in Collaborative Family Work and then worked with at least one family at a family welfare agency for at least six sessions of family work. The students were aged between 21 and 65, and none had any prior experience of family therapy. The agency provided services free of charge to disadvantaged families. In total, 24 students worked with twelve families (the students worked in pairs as co-counsellors) for a minimum of six to a maximum of twelve sessions, each lasting 45 minutes to one hour. All families who were referred to the students completed the minimum six-week intervention, with one exception when the family withdrew after the first session. Another family was then referred and the students concerned completed the work with the new family. Most of the families involved were also clients of other services, and were referred to the family welfare agency by child protection, juvenile justice and mental health. Four students also used the model on a similar basis in juvenile justice, where the students carried out a series of single case studies, each with positive outcomes in both client and worker evaluations (e.g. Trotter, Cox & Crawford 2002).

The model was also used with a mixed group of welfare professionals in an evaluation project funded by the Department of Justice in Victoria, Australia (Trotter 1997b). A two-day training course in the model was offered to a mixed group of school counsellors and youth workers. Nineteen participants who remained in the project and used the model had a range of professional qualifications, but few had specific qualifications or training in working with families. Those participating in the project worked with families on a range of issues—for example, family breakdown, truancy and criminal offending. In several instances where young people initially presented with family communication problems, child abuse became apparent as the family work progressed.

The workers completed an average of four sessions per client family, and each worker indicated that they worked with between two and nine families. The workers completed a questionnaire, six to eighteen months after completing the training course, regarding the relevance and usefulness of the model to their work and the extent to which they were able to help families. All but one of the nineteen workers said that they found the family intervention either totally or very successful with the families with whom they had worked.

Another project undertaken during 2007 and 2008 involved offering interventions to families following referral to the Gain Respect Increase Personal Power (GRIPP) program from a Children's Court. Cases were adjourned pending young people's involvement in family counselling and another group program. If they successfully completed the family counselling and the group sessions, they would return to court and their cases would be dismissed or adjourned. If they failed to complete the sessions, they would be sentenced in relation to the original offence. The young people and their families were offered six to twelve sessions of Collaborative Family Work and each of the counsellors received two days of training in the model plus ongoing supervision.

A further project is currently being undertaken in the juvenile justice system, whereby young people on juvenile justice orders are offered Collaborative Family Work in juvenile detention as part of their probation supervision. This is an ongoing project.

While hundreds of families have completed Collaborative Family Work interventions, at this stage we have collected only 36 formal client evaluations of the program (Trotter 2010). These evaluations are from the four projects referred to above. They include 28 families. In most cases, the family completed the evaluation as a group at the end of the intervention, and agreed on the score given for each question. In the other cases, individual family members decided to do their own evaluations.

The responses from family members have been positive, with most saying that they had benefited from the intervention.

- We asked the family members: 'On the whole, how are you getting along now compared with when you first began treatment here?' Seventy per cent of the family members said they were getting on much better, with 23 per cent saying they were getting on better. Only one of the 36 family members felt that things were worse after the family sessions.

- We found similar responses to the question: 'Consider the one problem you most wanted the worker to help you with. How is this problem now compared with how it was when you first started treatment here?' Eighty-three per cent of the family members said that the problem was either much better or no longer present. No one felt that the problem was worse and only 14 per cent felt that it was the same.

- We also asked: 'On the whole how would you rate the extent to which you benefited from the service?' with similar positive results. Seventy-two per cent said that they had benefited considerably, while 5 per cent of the family members said they could not have done without it. The remainder all felt that they had benefited from the family work.

Overall, most clients believed they were assisted by the service.

- Most clients felt that the service lasted the right amount of time.

- Most clients also indicated that they understood what their workers were trying to do.

- The aspects of the intervention that clients indicated they found most helpful included the worker's attempts to help them understand what was happening in their relationship, the workers' attempts to help them concentrate on specific problems or goals for them to work on, and following through at home with solutions worked out during the session.

Chapter summary

This chapter has argued that Collaborative Family Work has considerable research support. The model is based on research about what works and what doesn't in human services work. Each of the steps and practices in the model has substantial research support as an effective way to work. I pointed to the research support for problem-solving models and for problem-solving work with families in a range of different settings. It was acknowledged that problem-solving models vary, and that the effectiveness of any intervention is dependent on the way it is carried out and the individual skills of the workers. Nevertheless, Collaborative Family Work is based in 'what works' principles, and has been shown to be an effective way of working by workers who have basic skills in building alliances with clients.

The chapter also outlined the relatively small-scale evaluations undertaken on the Collaborative Family Work model. What do these evaluations tell us? First, they show that the model can be used with a wide variety of different families involved in the human services. The family members involved have included people from many different cultural backgrounds, including refugee families, Indigenous families and families where gender roles and expectations are very different from those of the workers. Family members have also included young people and adults with intellectual or learning disabilities, with acquired brain injury and with serious drug addictions. The work has typically been undertaken with poorly functioning families with whom human services workers work on a daily basis.

Second, the evaluations suggest that professional workers—even students—with limited experience of working with families can use this model with families in the welfare and criminal justice systems. While many of those using the model had skills and qualifications in one-to-one work, few had been involved in family work before using this model. Third, it has shown that family members who have participated in Collaborative Family Work generally have been satisfied with the experience. Most believed that the intervention had helped them considerably, and few—if any—felt that it made things worse.

A controlled and methodologically rigorous research study funded through the Australian Research Council is currently being undertaken with juvenile justice clients and their families in New South Wales, Australia. This study is examining family members' responses to the model and further offending by the young people involved. It is anticipated that the results of this study will shed further light on the effectiveness of the model.

The chapter pointed out that the model is not a traditional family therapy model, although it uses some family therapy techniques. It is a partnership model that aims to help family members to solve their problems. The worker acts as a coach for families to improve their communication and discuss issues in a rational and non-threatening manner.

I commented earlier on my own experiences over 20 years working as a child protection worker, a family welfare worker and a criminal justice supervisor. I often felt that the best way to address the problems of my clients was by working with their family group. When I did work with family groups, however, I did not feel that I had an appropriate model to help me structure the work. I felt that my work with families lacked a sense of purpose and direction. The rest of this book is devoted to helping workers, who may or may not be experienced family workers, to gain a sense of direction and purpose in their work with family groups.

4
Preparing families for family work and developing ground rules

As discussed in Chapter 1, family members may be involved in family work on a voluntary basis, they may be semi-voluntary and sometimes their participation is involuntary. On some occasions, family members have a problem and may approach an agency as a group seeking family work. At other times, an individual family member may approach an agency seeking family work on the understanding that other family members will be agreeable to participating—or can be persuaded to take part. On other occasions, a professional human services worker may feel that the best way to address issues faced by an individual client is through work with the family group, and the client and family members may be persuaded to be involved partly because of the authority of the worker.

Sometimes, a family may be court-ordered into counselling. This is often the case where courts deliberate over custody and other issues relating to divorce and separation. Family members may be forced into accepting family counselling services as a result of court directions or orders. This sometimes occurs in work with young offenders, and I referred in the previous chapter to a program where young offenders were referred to Collaborative Family Work following a court appearance and having been found guilty of an offence. While the young person and the family had to agree to be involved in the family work, their participation was largely involuntary because if they did not undertake the family work, the young person faced the possibility of a more severe penalty.

In many cases in work with families in human service settings such as child protection, probation, addictions, mental health or in schools—even when clients themselves seek family therapy or counselling—there is ambivalence on the part of the family members. Even when family members visit a family welfare agency seeking family work, one or more of the family members may be apprehensive about the decision to seek assistance. Even when family members are agreeable, when they have had family work before and when they understand what is involved, they may be apprehensive about the worker and the nature of the family work. They might, for example, be concerned about certain issues that they may not wish to share with professional workers.

Regardless of the apparent motivation of the clients, the role of the professional worker is to help family members to feel comfortable and optimistic about the potential of family work to help them. There is some research suggesting that it is difficult to disentangle the motivation of clients from the style and skills of the worker (Jones & Alcabes 1993; Loneck 1995). In fact, in our child protection study (Trotter 2004), we found that clients had better outcomes if they thought that their worker believed they could change rather than if they (the client) believed they could change. In other words, the worker's belief in the client was more important than the client's belief in themselves in terms of client outcome.

Therefore, it is important that in the preparation stages of family work the worker seeks 'buy-in' from the clients. The role of the worker in preparing family members for family work can be crucial to the motivation to continue, and it can provide the background to a successful intervention. In many respects, the family intervention begins at the time the possibility of family work is raised with any family member. Each conversation from then on, whether it is with the primary client or other family members, may influence the subsequent family work process and outcome. There are a number of ways in which workers can help the process of initial 'buy-in' from clients.

On some occasions, the initial discussions will be done on an individual basis. A worker may first ask a young person whether they would be agreeable to family work and the worker would then discuss what is involved with the young person. Between the young person and the worker, they may then decide to approach another family member—the young person's mother, for example. The worker and the young person may do that together or, alternatively, the worker may approach the mother separately. Or the young person might prefer to approach the mother directly before she has any contact with the worker. The order in which family members are approached can be worked out in a constructive way between the primary client and the worker.

Regardless of who is involved in the initial conversation, there are a number of issues that will be of interest to the client or clients. Ideally, these issues will be raised by clients as the discussion about the process of the family work progresses. In most cases, however, the workers will need to raise these issues as they attempt to help the client or clients understand how the family work will occur. Some of these issues are outlined below.

Has the client had family therapy or family counselling or any other type of family work before?

If the client has had family work before, the worker will want to understand the nature of the previous intervention: When did they do the family work? With whom? What was the nature of the work? Was it helpful? Which aspects were helpful? Which were unhelpful? How many sessions were there? How long did they last? Did the client finish the sessions? By understanding the nature of the previous intervention, the worker can gain a picture of the way the client understands family work and what they might expect in relation to the family work that is being offered. The worker can then clarify how the Collaborative Family Work model differs from the client's experience of family work.

Who will be involved?

The process of deciding who is to be approached may take some discussion with the primary client. This discussion represents the beginning of the collaborative process between the worker and the client—a process that will be continued when the family sessions start. The worker asks the client to talk about the advantages and disadvantages of involving different family members and whether or not they might be agreeable.

It may be valuable for the workers to do a family genogram so that they have a picture of who might be involved and can then discuss who should be invited to the sessions. The genogram is a graphic representation of the family, and may include details about family history, interpersonal relationships and legal relationships. An example of a genogram that can be used in Collaborative Family Work is shown in Figure 4.1.

Figure 4.1: Genogram

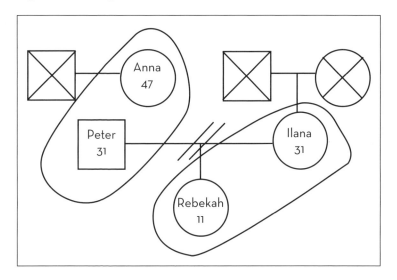

The mother, Ilana (31), lives with her daughter, Rebekah (11), and there are no other children. Rebekah's father, Peter (31), lives separately and Ilana never sees him. Rebekah, however, has contact with him. Ilana's parents are deceased. Peter's mother, Anna (47), is alive and has contact with Peter; however, Peter's father is deceased.

Generally, if the family members are agreeable, involved

in family dynamics and there is no evidence of abuse, violence or intimidation towards other family members, then they should be encouraged to be involved. People often ask how many family members it is advisable to work with at any one time. Collaborative Family Work has been done with up to eight family members, although there can be logistical difficulties involved in managing a large group and the process of working through individual problem lists may be time-consuming and not always relevant to all involved. There are advantages in keeping the group to three or four family members. If more than four people are to be involved in the sessions, the workers should be clear that there is a good reason for each person to be involved.

It should be made clear to family members that it is not appropriate to come along just to see what is involved or to attend one or two sessions but not others. There may be occasions when those involved might decide to invite a family member to attend one or two sessions for a specific purpose. For example, it may become apparent as the family work progresses that addressing a particular issue—say, where a young person should live—would be more easily done if both parents were involved in that discussion. A mother or father who had not participated to date might be invited to participate for one session to discuss this issue.

Will anyone know what goes on in the sessions?

Clients may be concerned that information about the family that emerges in the sessions could be divulged to others. For example, a mother might be concerned that if she undergoes family work, her son will pass confidential information on to his father. Or a father might be worried that if he is involved in the family work, his illegal drug use might be raised and passed on to other family members. It is important to have a discussion about the limits of confidentiality in sessions. In some of the families where Collaborative Family Work has been used, child abuse has been revealed during the sessions. On some occasions, this has related to past sexual abuse by a parent or relative who is not in the sessions but on other occasions it has related directly to past sexual or physical abuse of children or partners by family members who are participating in the family work sessions. It is important that those participating in the sessions understand that there may be limits to confidentiality and what those limits are.

Whose side is the worker on?

Sometimes young people in particular may be concerned that if they were involved in the family work, they will be blamed for things in the same way that they may be blamed by family members at home. They may be concerned that the worker will join with the family in blaming the young person or that, even if the worker is supportive to the young person, the other family members will not take a reasonable and even-handed approach to the family work. It is important that if the young person or other family members feel this way, it is discussed before the family work commences. If the issue cannot be resolved, it may signify that the family work is inappropriate.

It may also be that a young person is concerned that the family work will interfere with the relationship that they have with the worker who is proposing to do the family work. The young person may need reassurance that the level and nature of individual contact between the worker and client will remain the same once family work commences. The worker needs to be clear about the extent to which they will have contact with other family members outside the regular family work sessions. This will vary on an individual basis; however, the family work may be compromised if one or two family members choose to discuss issues between sessions with the workers, particularly if the content of those discussions is not open to other family members. It is certainly not uncommon for family members to ring workers before or after sessions, saying to the worker: 'I thought I should ring you before we meet as a family because there is something I think you should know but I don't want to say it in front of my son.' It should be clear to family members whether workers are agreeable to be involved in conversations between sessions and, if they are involved, whether the content of these conversations will be confidential.

There may be occasions when it is vital that individual family members feel free to talk confidentially to workers between sessions. I mentioned earlier that the family work may lead to issues being exposed that lead one family member to feel intimidated by another family member. Discussions may, for example, reveal past sexual or physical abuse, or other situations where one family member may need some protection. The worker may be the most appropriate person for the client to turn to in these situations. So while the smooth progress of the family work may sometimes be compromised by confidential discussions taking place between family work sessions, in some cases this may be necessary.

Rather than discuss the complexities of this issue in the preparation stage, it may be more appropriate to refer to the general principles of openness but explain that there may be exceptions to this in certain circumstances. Should an issue of abuse or another issue arise during the family work sessions, which necessitates confidential discussion with the worker, then this issue can be clarified further with family members at the time.

How long will it take?

Family members will want to know just what they are agreeing to in terms of the frequency and duration of the family work sessions. Before the family work begins, the worker should be clear about what is expected from family members in terms of how often and for what period they are expected to attend. While there may be occasions when family members must miss sessions, and times when having a session with parents alone or with a young person alone may be valuable, it is unlikely to be helpful if different family members attend different sessions and if the workers cannot be sure who will be present at the sessions at any given time.

Where will the family work take place?

If the sessions are to be held in the family home, is there a suitable room where the family and the workers can meet? Is there a time when everyone can get together? And is the home conducive to the family work? Dogs and cats, telephones, televisions, computer games, visitors and thoroughfares are not conducive to effective work with families. Some discussion about this with family members may head off potential issues later on.

What about other services?

Family members involved in the social services system are often involved with other services. It is not uncommon for an individual family to have contact with many professional workers. In our child protection study (Trotter 2004), for example, 10 per cent of the clients reported that they had contact with ten or more agencies: child protection, juvenile justice, adult corrections, offender support agencies, youth workers, family support workers, mental health services, drug treatment workers, financial counsellors, nursing services, school counsellors.

This raises two issues in relation to family work. The first is whether family work is likely to overlap with other services and leave clients with some degree of confusion about how to deal with their issues. Second, are the other professionals involved with the family aware of the family work, and do they support the work being carried out? The issue of working with other agencies is a complex one, and there has been criticism of case management as inefficient and disjointed (Steib & Blome 2004; Turner 2010). Suffice to say that in helping family members prepare for family work, some discussion with clients about other agencies and the services they provide may help the family worker/s to provide a service that complements other services.

What will happen in the sessions?

Reference was made earlier to the need to discuss with family members whether they had experienced family work or family therapy before. Family members who have not experienced family work previously are unlikely to have an accurate picture of what will be involved. Similarly, family members who have been through the experience of family therapy may, as discussed earlier, have built up a set of expectations about what will be involved. It should be explained to the individual family members that the family work will involve family members talking about what concerns they have, discussing those issues, deciding what they would like to change and working out ways to change them. Families will be coached in a method of solving problems in a way that is not blaming or threatening.

Can you really help us?

In workshops I conduct to teach professional workers the Collaborative Family Work model, I often ask the workers what they would like to know about a professional helper if they were personally seeking help. They usually respond by saying that they would like to know about the qualifications of the worker, what approach the worker takes to the work, whether the worker has helped people before, whether they were successful and whether they could be guaranteed confidentiality. The workshop participants feel that knowing these things would make them feel more comfortable and more inclined to use the services of the person offering help. It would also help to develop the credibility of the worker and the trust of the client.

When asked whether it is very different for their clients, they reflect on this and most say 'not much'. Clients may want less detail about the approach of the worker, and knowing that the worker has a degree in social work, psychology, youth work or family therapy may not mean a lot to many family members. Nevertheless, for family members, confidence in the ability of the worker to help is vital to a good start and a good intervention. The willingness of the worker to talk about the model and about how it has worked for other clients, the worker's confidence in the ability of the model to help and their qualifications to carry it out will all contribute to developing credibility with family members. This is consistent with the research that supports the importance of role clarification in work in human services (Trotter 2004, 2006; Videka-Sherman 1998).

Preparing families for family work is an essential part of the Collaborative Family Work model, so it is important that time is devoted to it. There is some evidence that human services workers tend to skip over preparation and role clarification issues (Bourgeon et al. 2010; Trotter 2004, 2010); however, there is also evidence that they are important to achieving good outcomes. The best results will be achieved when workers work systematically through the different stages of the model, including preparing the family—albeit in a flexible manner, as discussed in Chapter 3.

A summary of the issues that should be covered in preparing families for family work is provided in Figure 4.2.

Figure 4.2: Preparing families for family work

- What are the clients' expectations?
- Why are there two workers?
- Who will be involved?
- Will anyone else know what goes on in sessions?
- Can individual family members have discussions with the worker between sessions?
- Whose side is the worker on?
- Where will the family work take place?
- How long will it take?
- What will the family work involve?
- What about other services ?
- Can you really help?

The first session

In most cases, the workers will have at least met the family members before the first session; however, on some occasions the worker may not have met all family members. There may also be occasions when workers will not have met any of the family members prior to coming to the first session, particularly if the worker is employed by a family counselling agency where family members simply make an appointment to come in for family counselling or therapy.

Ideally, workers will have worked through the issues referred to earlier in this chapter and family members will be well prepared for the first session. In these instances, the workers may revisit the issues briefly and satisfy themselves that the family members have a clear picture of how the family work will be delivered. In situations where the workers have not had the opportunity to prepare the family, they will need to work through the issues with the family at the beginning of the first session.

The workers should then raise the issues referred to earlier. What previous experience do the family members have of family therapy? Who are the most suitable family members (or others) to involve in the family work? Does everyone have to attend every session? Is what goes on in sessions confidential? Are the workers neutral? How many sessions will there be and how long will they take? What will happen in the sessions and how can the workers help?

The focus at all stages of the family work is on the family members talking, rather than the workers, and as far as possible the first session should involve family members asking questions in order to understand the nature of the family work. The aim is for interaction with all family members involved.

Workers may wish to take some control over seating arrangements. While in many cases this will be difficult when working in the family home, there may be advantages in suggesting certain seating arrangements. From a practical point of view, it is best to separate siblings who tend to fight with each other, even if this behaviour seems to be good-natured. When the workers believe that two or more family members have a tendency to join together and exclude or blame another family member, then separating the two may help to avoid this happening in the sessions.

If two workers are involved in the family work, then the workers should outline how they will work together. They should explain that one worker will take the lead in each of the sessions and the other will summarise, and that the roles will be reversed at other times. They can also explain that they will be trying to model a healthy and productive way of working together and negotiating disagreements if and when they arise. If one worker has a particular relationship with a family member (as a case manager, for example), then the issues discussed earlier concerning contact between sessions and neutrality will also need to be highlighted.

The workers should also ensure that the family members understand the way in which the family sessions will work. Large sheets of paper with copies of the family problem structure might be taken by the workers to the family home or displayed in the workers' office. The workers should ensure that the family members understand the process of Collaborative Family Work.

Once the workers are satisfied that the family members have a clear understanding of what is involved (as distinct from being satisfied that they have explained what is involved), then they should move on to the first stage of the model: setting the ground rules.

Setting ground rules

The first step in the model, once the role clarification issues referred to above have been addressed, is for the family members to develop ground rules for the session. There are several reasons for developing ground rules.

First, they can provide guidelines and parameters for the participation in the family sessions for both family members and workers. It is not unusual for family members to interact in a consistently negative manner in their day-to-day lives. Many of the families who have been involved in our family work sessions report that they rarely if ever have positive and cooperative conversations. Their interactions are often characterised by abuse, disagreements and lack of respect. Shouting or attempts to bully each other are typical methods used by family members to get their own way or to settle disputes. The setting of ground rules for the sessions can make it clear from the outset that the method of interaction in the family work sessions will not be a replication of what happens at home. It can prevent or at least minimise the potential for arguments and abuse taking place in the family work sessions.

Second, in itself, setting ground rules with family members is a task that can and usually does lead to good outcomes. It is the beginning of the therapy. By working on the task of setting ground rules for the sessions, the family members are involved in working together and reaching agreement on a relatively non-threatening issue. The experience of developing the rules together can be the beginning of learning a new way of interacting. It begins the process of teaching communication skills.

Third, setting the ground rules for the sessions can carry over to the way family members interact at home. What they learn in the family sessions can influence their ongoing communication skills. The setting of the ground rules can also be a homework task, whereby family members think about or discuss the ground rules that should be used in the sessions. Again, this can contribute to improved communication among family members.

The worker should explain to the family that it will help the sessions to run smoothly if they agree on rules or guidelines for the way the sessions will operate. If the workers feel that the term 'ground rules' is problematic, it might be better to use terms such as guidelines or agreements or principles. Sometimes young people may associate the term 'rules' with school, and it can have negative connotations.

The workers should then ask the family members to suggest ground rules. This becomes the first family task. The workers may ask one family member to speak first. There may be advantages in asking the least powerful person to speak first—for example, a young person who has little influence in the family; this may give the message to the family that all members will be expected to participate. On the other hand, there may also be advantages in allowing the family members to decide who starts. This may be the least threatening approach for the family members, and the workers can then address issues of lack of participation at a later stage. Which is the best approach to take is a judgement the workers need to make on the basis of individual family circumstances.

Ideally, the family members will come up with ground rules and the workers can clarify their meaning and write them down. However, in practice the workers may need to suggest at least some of the ground rules to the family for their consideration. Some examples of ground rules taken from actual family sessions are outlined in Figure 4.3.

Figure 4.3: Examples of ground rules

- Family members should not shout at each other.
- Family members should show respect for each other and not interrupt when others speak.
- Family members should encourage each other.
- A talking stick should be used, and the only person who can speak is the person who currently holds the talking stick.
- One person talks at a time.
- Talk briefly so other people get a chance to talk—no one is to dominate the conversation.
- Everyone is encouraged to be honest and say what they believe while also respecting other people's feelings.
- If someone says they should do something, they should do it.
- Family members should not swear at each other.
- Anything that is said in the family work sessions will not be repeated to anyone outside the sessions.
- All family members will attend every session; however, if they are unable to, they will notify the worker.
- If anyone feels uncomfortable or angry or bullied during the session, they can leave for a short period.
- If anyone feels uncomfortable or angry or bullied, they should tell the others in the session how they are feeling.
- Family members can call for a break during the sessions if they feel they need a pause from proceedings.
- Between sessions, family members will not raise issues discussed in sessions in a negative way.
- The television will be turned off before sessions start and not turned on again until they finish.
- Phone calls will not be taken.
- If anyone comes to the door, they will be asked to come back later.
- No one is to fight with each other, even in a playful manner.
- Written records of ground rules, problems, goals and other documentation of the family work processes will be typed on large sheets of paper by the worker and brought to the family home so that they can be displayed in the room where the family work takes place.

As the rules are suggested by family members, the workers should ensure that all of the family members agree to them. On some occasions, it might be necessary for the family members to explain or expand on the rule when they suggest it. For example, in one family a mother was concerned that her children would tell their father about the sessions. In agreeing to the ground rules, it was emphasised that no information was to be passed on to the children's father.

As the rules are raised, it may be necessary for the workers to clarify meaning. For example, if someone suggests using a talking stick then some discussion can take place as to how this will work. It may be appropriate to explain that the talking stick will be passed on when the person talking has finished, and that the period of time it can be held for is limited to five minutes.

The worker should also take a role in ensuring that the ground rules are reasonable, and not used to scapegoat any individual. For example, some people swear as part of their daily conversation. It may be an ingrained habit and/or it may reflect limited language skills. In either case, to express oneself adequately without swearing might be very difficult. In this instance, the worker needs to take care that a ground rule to not allow swearing does not represent an attempt by other family members to scapegoat one member.

Sometimes family members ask: 'What happens if we don't follow the ground rules?' This raises the issue of who is responsible for ensuring that family members (and workers, for that matter) comply with the ground rules. The aim of Collaborative Family Work is to help family members to learn new ways of communicating and new ways of solving problems. On this basis, the family members develop the rules and they therefore hold the responsibility for ensuring that the rules are adhered to. This should involve a general group pressure to comply rather than any individual taking responsibility for enforcing the rules. If rules are consistently broken, then the workers should ask the family members to consider why this is occurring and whether or not the ground rules should be reviewed: do some family members not agree with them, or are they unable to carry them out? This is consistent with the non-blaming focus of this model.

The Collaborative Family Work model assumes a willingness by family members to participate in a power-sharing arrangement. No family member should dominate or control discussions around ground rules, problems or strategies. This can present problems for some families where one member perceives that they are the head of the family and expects to be in charge. Sometimes there are cultural expectations around this issue. Family members may have been raised in a culture that ascribes particular roles to family members whereby the father is viewed as the head of the family, children are not expected to challenge or question their parents and women are expected to play a role purely as mother and wife. It is important that workers are sensitive to the cultural expectations of the family members with whom they work. It is also important that in preparing families for Collaborative Family Work, workers spend time helping family members to understand the equal power-sharing arrangement involved in the model and ensure that there is a willingness to work in this way.

When the family members have agreed on the ground rules and they have been written down by the workers or by a family member, preferably on large piece of paper, this section of the model is finished for now. The workers should confirm as discussed above that the ground rules can be changed if they do not work or if anyone is unhappy with them; however, in the meantime these will form the basis on which the sessions will operate. The worker then takes the copy of the ground rules and, before the next session, types up the rules and brings the page to the next session, preferably blown up on a large laminated piece of paper that can be displayed for all to see in subsequent sessions. Figure 4.4 provides an example.

Figure 4.4: Ground rules as agreed by family members

Ground rules

- No shouting
- TV off
- Phones off
- Show respect
- No visitors—ask them to come back later
- Allow each other to speak
- Leave the room if you feel angry
- Come to the session on time

Generally, the role-clarification and ground rules discussions will occupy most of the first session. During the process of discussion, however, family issues inevitably will be raised by family members. When, for example, family members are asked to talk about their expectations, they will often comment that 'I am here because I want to do something about my son's terrible behaviour' or 'I expect that something can be done to stop the constant family conflict' or 'We somehow have to work out how we can live together'. When issues like this are raised, the workers should listen to what the family members have to say, but steer them back to the task at hand, whether it involves talking about roles and the nature of the family work or the ground rules. A typical comment might be: 'I would like you to hold that thought so that we can come back to it when we start identifying the issues which are of concern to you.' The worker can then point to the outline of the steps in the model that will have been given to family members during the preparation stages or in the early part of the first session.

At the conclusion of the first session (and later sessions), it can be valuable to give the family a session-based activity or task and/or a homework activity or task. As discussed in Chapter 7, tasks and strategies for the most part are used to address specific goals that have been identified by family members. However, facilitative tasks may also be used to provide a sense of direction or purpose or simply to improve family communication, even though they are not directed towards a specific problem or goal.

An example of a session-based task that might be used at the end of the first session might be:

> We have talked a lot about how the family work will operate and the ground rules we need to have in place to ensure that the sessions run smoothly. One issue that seems to have arisen is when the sessions will take place: Mario has work commitments, Mary does not like morning meetings and Dinath works in the mornings. So let's have a discussion about when we can meet using the ground rules we have just put in place.

The family members can then each present their preferences and a suitable time can be negotiated. This, along with the ground rules, begins the process of negotiation that the family work aims to develop.

Another facilitative session task that might be appropriate could be explained to the family members as follows:

> I have noticed that there is quite a lot of disagreement and anger between you, yet you have all chosen of your own free will to participate in the family work. This suggests to me that even though you are angry with each other, you actually care a lot about each other. I am wondering if we could try an activity before we finish up the session. I would like each of you to say something about what you like or admire about each other.

This particular task is probably used more than any other in Collaborative Family Work. It ends the session on a positive note and helps to balance any negativity involved in the discussions about problems. It is also a task which family members generally respond to. The fear of some workers that family members will not be able, or will choose not, to think of things they like about each other has rarely been realised in the Collaborative Family Work in which I have been involved.

It can also be valuable to give family members general facilitative home tasks or activities. Either of the session tasks could also be home tasks. Family members could be asked to think about what times they can make available for further sessions so that they fit in with the needs of other family members. They could also be asked to think about the things they like about each other with a view to presenting these at the beginning of the next session. In setting home tasks, care needs to be taken to ensure that the tasks are manageable, that they won't fuel family conflict in any way and that potential obstacles to their implementation are considered. In Chapter 7, details are provided in relation to developing session tasks and home tasks, and dealing with obstacles to carrying out the tasks. The point is being made here that it can be valuable to give family members one or two general tasks at the conclusion of the first session in order to foster positive feeling and to give a sense of direction, as well as to involve family members further.

Pro-social modelling

Reference was made in Chapter 3 to pro-social modelling. Pro-social modelling is one of the skills that workers use in the process of working with families or individuals, and that facilitates positive outcomes. It is worth emphasising pro-social modelling at this stage because, as discussed earlier, it is an important skill in human services work (Trotter 2006, 2012). It is vital that workers make use of the principles of pro-social modelling and reinforcement throughout the first and subsequent family work sessions. This involves the workers purposefully praising the positive actions and comments of the family members, congratulating the family members for their decision to be involved in family work, acknowledging the time and commitment involved and acknowledging the individual contributions made to the discussions. For example, the workers can acknowledge a family member when they listen to another family member, when they suggest ground rules, when they speak respectfully to another family member or when turn off their phone.

The workers can also acknowledge any pro-social comments family members make in relation to the reason they are involved in the justice or social services systems. For example, if the family work involves working with the family of a young offender and the young offender acknowledges that stealing cars is wrong or leads to negative consequences, the worker should reinforce this. If a mother in the child protection system talks about the importance of being home for her children, this can be reinforced by positive responses from the worker. If a child has attended school during the week and truancy has been a problem, then the worker should acknowledge this. At the end of the first session, and in subsequent sessions, the worker should congratulate the family members for coming to the session, reinforce that the decision to come is an indication of their interest in improving their family relationship and stress the importance of these relationships for family members.

Family functioning scale

The family functioning scale was referred to in Chapter 3. The scale should be completed in the first session, with each family member offering a rating. In one juvenile justice agency where extensive use has been made of this model, the staff has developed a kit to take with them to the family homes. The kit includes a copy of the family functioning scale and the family members are invited to place a plastic ant on the number on the scale to indicate their view about the family functioning. The ant is used because ants have a particular meaning in Aboriginal culture, and many of the juvenile justice clients in the region are Aboriginal. It also provides a fun way of carrying out the task.

The aim of filling out the family functioning scale is to find out the level of functioning of the family before Collaborative Family Work begins and as the family work progresses. It is best done early in the first session. If it is done later, after the family have discussed ground rules in a collaborative fashion, the family members' views about the level of functioning may be different from their earlier view. The scale can also be used to help develop goals and monitor progress of the family, as discussed in Chapter 3.

Set out below is an excerpt from a transcript of an interview between a worker in a family services agency, an 11-year-girl, Rebekah, and her mother, Ilana (whom we met in Chapter 4). The girl has been referred following truancy, difficulties at school and suspected stealing. The interview takes place in the family home. While it is common, as mentioned earlier, for two workers to be involved in Collaborative Family Work, in this case only one experienced worker is involved.

Worker:	Hi Rebekah.
Rebekah:	Hello.
Worker:	Hi Ilana, thanks for inviting me in. Have you done this sort of family counselling before? Do you know anything about it, Rebekah? When you were referred from the school, did they tell you anything about what would be involved?
Rebekah:	They just said that we would talk to a man.
Worker:	Yeah.
Rebekah:	They will come to my house.
Worker:	OK—did they explain what for?
Rebekah:	No.
Worker:	Just that someone would come and talk to you? What about you, Ilana? Have you done family counselling before?
Ilana:	No, I have just been to see the school counsellor a lot—she is always in trouble at

	school and they drag me up there at least once a week to tell me all the crap she has been doing at school and that's all—they said we need to see someone else.
Worker:	Did they say why they were referring you to me?
Ilana:	No, they just said we need to talk to someone. They have told us to do it a few times before but she has never wanted to come.
Worker:	Okay—but this time you are happy to be involved in it, Rebekah?
Rebekah:	Yes, because you came to our house.
Worker:	Okay—the other times you had to go to an office, did you? I have been told there are some problems between you and there are some problems at school, and the idea is for us to sort the problems out between us. Often it is very hard to sort the problems out unless you have a third person to help you work out what the problems are and what you can do about them.
Ilana:	I think it is pretty easy to see what the problems are—she doesn't listen to me and she is always in trouble.
Worker:	What we need to do is sort out how we are going to go about doing this and what sorts of rules we are going to have for the session.
Ilana:	Good luck, she won't stick to rules.
Worker:	Well, for all of us I mean—in terms of how we run the session. I know you have not done this sort of counselling before, but you have seen the school welfare people, Rebekah, and we will be doing the same sort of thing you have been doing with them but we will be doing it together.

Rebekah:	Yeah.
Worker:	Have you got any idea of the sorts of rules we would want to make to make sure everything works in this session? For example, we might want to make sure no one yells over the top of each other or those sorts of things. Have you got any ideas about this?
Ilana:	I don't want you to be disrespectful.
Worker:	Okay, sure.
Ilana:	I think she should listen to what you have to say.
Worker:	That we all should listen?
Ilana:	You have made this effort to come out to us so she should listen.
Worker:	I think it is a good idea to make a note of the rules we will have for the session—so one thing you are saying is we should listen to each other? When someone speaks we should not interrupt them?
Ilana:	Yes.
Rebekah:	Yes.
Worker:	What would be some other things?
Ilana:	Well, who are you going to tell about what has happened here? What is going to happen with the information?
Worker:	Okay, the things that we talk about here we wouldn't be talking about to other people?
Ilana:	Yes—I don't want Rebekah to go and tell people at school what might have happened.
Worker:	So if you talked about something personal, you wouldn't want Rebekah to go and talk about it. What do you think about that, Rebekah?
Rebekah:	I wouldn't want that either.
Worker:	You wouldn't want your mum to talk about

	what happened here—so everything that happens here is just between us?
Ilana:	So you think you can do that? You are not going to tell your dad?
Rebekah:	My dad?
Ilana:	You won't tell him what happens?
Rebekah:	No.
Worker:	The only problem with this is if there was something very serious, like if I found out that you were being hit or something like that, then it might be necessary to report it to someone else.
Ilana:	I don't hit her.
Worker:	No, I am not saying that. In sessions like this, everything can be confidential; however, if something comes up like a child being abused then it would be necessary to report it. I don't mean in this situation but just so you know how this works if something like that happens.
Ilana:	It doesn't.
Worker:	It doesn't—that's good. What other rules do you think we would want to have?
Rebekah:	Not sure.
Worker:	So we want to listen to each other and we don't want the things going outside this room.
Ilana:	Did you say not interrupting when the other one talks?
Worker:	Okay—not interrupting when the other person is talking.
Ilana:	Not sure of any others.
Rebekah:	Can't think of any others.
Ilana:	So what will happen if we break those?
Worker:	Well, these are just guidelines so we get off to a good start. If they are not working we

	can discuss how we can make them work and we might have to change them. This is what we have so far—we have to listen to each other; it is just between us; we are not going to interrupt each other. I think it is a good idea in these sessions to not put each other down—not say nasty things to each other.
Ilana:	Did you hear that? (to Rebekah)
Worker:	What we don't want is to blame the other person and say horrible things in these sessions so we will try to be positive—what do you think about that?
Ilana:	We can try.
Worker:	So now we have these rules here for the sessions—what do you think? (showing the rules written on a large piece of paper)

- Allow the other person to speak without interrupting.
- What happens in the session stays in the session.
- Respect each other.
- Listen to each other.
- Don't say nasty things to each other.

Ilana:	Yes.
Rebekah:	Yes.
Worker:	So we can talk about these further, but these are just for now and as we go we can add more rules if we want, but use these as a basis.
Rebekah:	Yes.
Worker:	Good. Now I want you to tell me a little bit about why you think I have come here, Rebekah.
Rebekah:	Because I get into trouble at school 'cause my friends—not really my friends, but the kids at school—tease me a lot.

Worker:	Okay.
Rebekah:	And my mum never lets me see my father.
Worker:	I see.
Rebekah:	And I don't like that. I like seeing my father.
Worker:	So the teachers at school thought if I came along to see you we could sort out some of these problems with your mum at least—and you thought that was a good idea, at least if the person comes to your house and you don't have to go somewhere else. Well, I hope we can sort out these things because the idea is to sort out problems with your mum and hopefully things will improve at school as well. What about you, Ilana? What were your expectations—what were you hoping to get out of this?
Ilana:	I was hoping you could sort out her behaviour a bit because she doesn't do anything around the house and we have screaming matches every night and every morning because she doesn't want to do anything—and the Dad issue is a whole different problem.
Worker:	So it seems like there are some real issues between you, and you felt having this counselling could be helpful?
Ilana:	Yes, I want her to get through school and I don't want to be fighting with her all the time—we weren't doing much good for ourselves.
Rebekah:	I don't like school.
Worker:	You don't like school? Well, we will come back to that. Anyway, I think you have made a very good decision because working together on these things can very helpful. I have had a

lot of situations where people have problems, and talking about them and working through what the problems are and how you can deal with them has been very helpful. I want to talk to you now a bit about the process I am wanting to use with you. I will show this to you (worker shows a sheet of paper with problem-solving outline).

- Rules for sessions
- Identify problems
- Decide what to work on first
- Goals
- Explore the problems
- Strategies

We will work on this. Can you read it, Rebekah? We have talked about ground rules. Then we will talk about problems or things that are worrying you. We can talk about any of your problems as you see them—can you follow that, Rebekah?

Ilana: Do you know what that second one means?

Rebekah: No.

Worker: We are going to discuss all your problems, the things that are worrying you—that's what that means, and work out what you would like to achieve and then work out some methods of achieving it—anyway, as we go I will try and explain to you what we are doing.

Ilana: Is it going to take a long time?

Worker: It would usually take six or eight sessions— how do you feel about that?

Ilana: Well I suppose it is up to Rebekah.

Worker: You don't have to do this, Rebekah, if you

> Rebekah: think it is not working for you—if it is not
> helping you.
> If Mum lets me see Dad more, then I will
> come.
> Worker: Okay—so if it seems like it is helping, you will
> come. We can put this down as one of the
> rules if you like, that you don't have to be
> involved. I hope you will be involved and I
> hope you will give it a good go, but you will
> not be forced to come.
> Ilana: Yeah, but what happens if she doesn't come
> and still mucks up at school?
> Worker: What I hope is that it is helpful, Rebekah. I
> would like you to be involved but you don't
> have to and that applies to you too, Ilana. If
> you think it is not being helpful, what I would
> like you to say to me is this is not helpful and
> we can sort it out. I can come to your house
> every week for six weeks and I can come at
> this time and I hope you find it helpful.

This interview focuses on the ground rules and some beginning discussion of the presenting problems. It is an extract from a longer interview and does not cover everything that went on in the first session. For example, it does not cover the introduction of the rating scales and it does not include facilitative tasks—for example, identifying what family members like about each other—which are commonly used in the first session. (Facilitative tasks are discussed in Chapter 7.) It does, however, give a general idea of how the first session might be conducted. It identifies the ground rules, helps to clarify the purpose of the family work and begins to ease the family members' anxieties about how the sessions will progress.

One issue that is often raised when this case study is discussed with practitioners relates to Ilana's habit of interrupting and her negative comments about Rebekah. The worker chooses to ignore these, even though they are inconsistent with the ground rules that are being developed. The worker took the view that improving the method of interacting between mother and daughter was best done through a gradual process, and through purposively ignoring the comments rather than constant challenging.

Chapter summary

This chapter has begun the description of the step-by-step process of Collaborative Family Work. It identified issues that should be discussed in preparing family members for family work. It referred to the questions: Has the client had family therapy or family counselling or any other type of family work before? Who will be involved? Will anyone else know what arises in the sessions? Whose side is the worker on? Who should attend? How long will it take? What about other services? What will happen in the sessions? Can you really help us? Ideally, these issues are addressed with each family member before the family work session begins; however they are commonly revisited at the start of the session and in some instances they are mostly addressed within the first session. It was pointed out that it is vital that these issues are addressed in order to help family members to engage in the process.

The chapter then discussed the development of ground rules, and it was highlighted that this represents the beginning of a process of developing cooperative communication between family members. The family functioning scale was discussed, and the importance of the ongoing use of pro-social modelling skills by workers was emphasised. In the next chapter, we move on to the next step in the process: identifying problems.

5
Identifying issues to work on and focusing on strengths

This chapter outlines the next step in the family work process: helping family members to identify areas of concern to them. It outlines a process by which each family member can develop a list of concerns and then can be encouraged to reframe these concerns using non-blaming language. It also suggests ways in which client and family strengths can be incorporated into these discussions. Methods of dealing with situations where family members are in denial are discussed. Reference is also made to how workers can use pro-social modelling techniques to respond to issues that may emerge in family work sessions—for example, family violence, sexual abuse or interpersonal dominance. Again, practical real-life (but de-identified) examples are provided to illustrate how this work can be done.

This stage in the model—identifying problems, or

things that family members would like to change—commonly begins in the second session, although (as explained earlier) the timing of each of the stages of the model varies according to the needs of individual families, the style of individual workers and the number of sessions of Collaborative Family Work that are offered.

Review the last session

Whatever stage the family is at in the Collaborative Family Work process, the second session—like all sessions—begins with an acknowledgement by the worker of the presence of the family members. The presence of the family members at the session reflects, at least to some degree, a willingness to work on issues and a level of concern about improving family relationships. This can be emphasised with family members.

The family members are then asked to complete the family functioning rating sheets. This can be done quickly; however, the workers should take note of any changes between sessions. If things have improved, the worker can ask why and reinforce the benefits that might be showing already from the family work. If things have deteriorated, then the workers can also ask why and ensure that the issues are followed up later in the session.

The workers then review what has been done so far. They display the ground rules on a large sheet of paper and ask the family members whether they are still happy with them. If anyone feels that any of the ground rules are not suitable, or they have thought of more ground rules during the week, then the ground rules may be discussed again. If everyone is agreeable, new rules may be added or the rules may be amended.

If homework tasks or activities have been set in the previous meeting, then these should be reviewed. If tasks have been carried out, then the workers can discuss with the family members what occurred and how the family members responded. For example, a task may have been set in the previous session to think about the ground rules and come to the next session with any new rules. Or a task might have been set to identify the things that family members like about each other, and this can be discussed early in the meeting.

If the task has been carried out and the response from family members was positive, the workers can ask the family members to describe how the task was undertaken and the response from each person involved in the task. If, for example, a listening task was used, then the family members can be asked to describe how they felt about being listened to and how they found the process of listening to another person. A discussion could be held about whether this technique can be used more often and when it might be appropriate to use it.

On the other hand, if the task was not carried out, a discussion can be held regarding why it was not carried out. Was the task not clearly defined? Was it too hard? For example, did the family member who was listening really understand how to listen to someone else? Did the speaker or the listener not really agree to the task or did they think it was an inappropriate task? The worker can explore in this way why the task was not carried out and the task can then either be discarded or redefined so that it can be attempted again.

Perhaps the task was carried out but the response from those involved was poor. Perhaps one person listened but another person didn't. The workers might then ask similar questions to these in relation to tasks not carried out—for example, was the task unsuccessful because obstacles to its implementation had not been discussed sufficiently beforehand? Chapter 7 discusses tasks in more detail. The point being made here is that tasks that are set should be reviewed at the beginning of each session.

Problem identification

Following the review of the last session, the worker again shows the family work model to the family members and explains that they are now in the 'identifying problems' stage of the model. The worker then asks each family member to talk about things that are of concern to them, and writes them down as the client talks. It may take five to ten minutes for each family member to talk about their issues, and it can be explained to the other family members that they will get their turn but that they need to give each other the time to speak.

The worker then asks one family member to begin—perhaps the least powerful person, as discussed in Chapter 4. The aim at this stage is to gain a thorough picture of the issues facing the family members. The worker may need to prompt the family members if they are unsure of what to say or if they become focused only on one issue. The worker may have a checklist of issues in their mind which they may use to prompt the family members. The worker should encourage the participants to talk about general issues: school/work; finances; health; peer group; drug use; extended family; girlfriends/boyfriends or partners.

The worker should encourage the clients to be specific. If, for example, a family member says 'We fight all the time', the interviewer may ask about who fights with whom, what they fight about and whether the flights are physical or verbal. The worker should also encourage the clients to express the issues in non-blaming language. For example, a mother commented in relation to her son:

'Dimitrie stays out until all hours of the night and never tells me what he is doing or where he is.'

This was reframed by the worker into non-blaming language with the focus on the mother owning the problem:

'I am worried about Dimitrie staying out late because I don't know what he is doing and I feel I am losing touch with him.'

To take another example: A mother commented:

'Felicia constantly argues with me—she takes no notice of anything I say. She is never home, and I am sick of it.'

The worker helped the mother to reframe this into a statement about how she felt:

'I feel that I am failing as a mother and I am so disappointed that Felicia and I can't seem to have any positive conversations and I worry about her safety when she goes out.'

As each family member speaks, the worker writes down the problems. If there is only one worker, then the worker writes the problems down. If there are two workers, then the second worker writes the notes. If possible, this is done on a large piece of paper so that the family members can see what is written. In the example above, the workers felt that the statements referred to were too long to include in the mother's problem list and were abbreviated for the problem list to: 'worried about where Dimitrie goes'; 'no positive conversations' and 'worried about Felicia's safety'.

After the first family member has identified their problems, the worker goes through the list and explains that this is the client's list and can be changed at any time. The client is then invited to comment on whether it reflects accurately what they have said and whether they would like to make any changes to what has been written down.

The problems that may be raised are many and varied. Some common examples include: inability to have positive conversations with other family members; constantly receiving negative comments from other family members; arguments over household chores such as setting the table, mowing the lawn, cleaning up a bedroom; concern about drug use of a family member; insufficient privacy; favouritism of one child; and limitations on contact with a non-custodial parent.

A summary of some guidelines for identifying problems is shown in Figure 5.1.

Figure 5.1: Problem identification

> - Each family member states what they see as the issues of concern to them.
> - Start with least powerful member?
> - Other members may only seek clarification.
> - Focus on current issues.
> - Canvass issues not raised (e.g. work, finances, peers, school, drugs, other family members, recreation).
> - Write the problems for each family member on a board/ paper.
> - Express problems in non-blaming terms—reframing by worker as necessary.
> - Worker suggests issues the worker feels are important but not acknowledged by clients.
> - Identify strengths.

Shared problems

The problems should be listed under each family member's name. The workers then consider which of the problems are common to all or most family members. For example, it may be that all family members have identified a problem with frequent arguments over carrying out household chores, such as cleaning a bedroom, preparing dinner or washing dishes. Another column can be devoted to the common family problems. An example of a problem list is provided at the end of this chapter.

Problems unrelated to family issues

I have suggested that the workers should canvass a range of issues with family members. It may be, however, that some issues are not related to family dynamics. For example, a mother may be having trouble at work. This may be indirectly related to the family difficulties inasmuch as her unhappiness at work makes it more difficult to cope at home. It may also impact on the family if she were to lose her job. This issue is not likely to be a priority for the family work sessions; nevertheless, if it is raised it can be put on the mother's list. It may be that a family discussion about this issue could help to develop strategies that the mother might use at work. It could be that the family working together on such an issue would help the mother with both the issue and family relationships more generally.

While for the most part family work focuses on common family issues, it is up to the family members to identify problems, and there may be instances where individual issues are appropriate targets for discussion. The self-guided nature of the problem-solving process is at the heart of Collaborative Family Work, and if family members wish to pursue an issue that appears peripheral to the family dynamics, then they may be doing this for a good reason.

What if the clients don't identify the real issues?

It may be that the workers feel there are important issues that the family members have not acknowledged—for example, the drug use or dominating attitude of one of the family members. In such a situation, the workers might ask the family members whether there are other issues and prompt them in relation to issues which they have not identified. A worker might say: 'Are there any issues relating to drug use in the family?' or 'It seems to me that in this family some people don't get much of a chance to express their opinion—does anyone feel that way?'

The family members should not be pressed on this. The list of issues is each individual family member's list and this must be respected. Nevertheless, the workers might raise the issue again at an appropriate time if they feel that there continues to be an important issue that has not been brought out into the open. It is important to remember, however, that there may be times when the 'real' issues are too difficult for family members to handle or they do not have sufficient trust in the workers to raise it with them. There may be advantages in working on less emotional and less threatening issues in the initial stages of the work. Collaborative Family Work aims to help family members to develop positive methods of communicating with each other, whether it is through addressing 'real' or peripheral issues.

This is well illustrated by a case example. This instance involved Collaborative Family Work with a couple. It was apparent to the workers that the couple shared an unequal relationship, with the male partner dominating the female partner. Consistent with the model, the workers raised this issue but neither party wished to include it in their problem list. The family continued to work on an issue that the couple both saw as important—although the workers saw it as something of a side issue: how they could reach agreement on a plan to bring the male partner's ageing mother from Lithuania to live with them.

As the sessions progressed and they discussed this and other issues, the clients began to develop more trust in the ability of the workers to help them with their problems. In the sixth session, the woman said that she was scared to disagree with her partner on a number of issues and that she had been reluctant to tell her partner that she did not wish to spend many years of her life caring for her partner's mother. She said she had been considering leaving the relationship because of this. She then asked to put the issue of her fear of disagreeing with her partner on her problem list. The workers were then able to work through this issue with the couple, and put strategies in place to address it. In the final evaluation, both partners said that they could not have done without the family work, and told the workers the problems they had worked on were no longer present.

Focus on practical 'here and now' issues

While some family therapy models are concerned with trans-generational and early childhood experiences, the Collaborative Family Work model focuses on current 'here and now' issues. When clients raise non-specific problems such as depression, low self-esteem, anxiety or guilt, for example, they should be broken down into more tangible concerns. For example, a young woman who expresses concern about feeling bad about herself and having low self-esteem might be asked to talk about why she has low self-esteem. It might be possible to relate this to not having friends, not having work, feeling stigmatised by being on a court order or feeling inadequate because she has no money. Rather than identifying low self esteem as an issue, it may be possible to define the issue as 'I feel like I am failing as a mother when my daughter is so rude to me' or 'I have felt terrible since I broke off with my girlfriend'.

The focus of the model is therefore on 'here and now' issues rather than on past incidents that cannot be changed. Nevertheless, there may be times when past issues are so overwhelmingly important to family members that they need to be addressed. While the focus of Collaborative Family Work is on 'here and now' issues, those 'here and now' issues may be directly related to past incidents.

Another example illustrates this point. A young woman, Romana, and her mother were undertaking Collaborative Family Work. They had not spoken to each other for more than a year since Romana had run away from home and was subsequently placed in a residential care facility because she refused to live with her mother. She was asked to leave the residential facility because of her violence towards other residents. Her mother agreed to Collaborative Family Work to try to resolve the issue of accommodation for Romana. Some weeks into the sessions, Romana became very upset and told her mother that she would never forgive her for allowing her father to sexually assault her when she was 12 years old. While this was a past event, it was uppermost in the mind of Romana and her feelings about it were directly influencing her relationship with her mother. For this reason, the workers encouraged Romana and her mother to identify this as a problem. Through the Collaborative Family Work process, mother and daughter were able to resolve a lot of Romana's feelings about her mother relating to this issue. Both Romana and her mother provided positive evaluations of the family work, and Romana subsequently returned to live with her mother and sought sexual assault counselling. In this instance, Romana's resentment towards her mother was a current 'here and now' issue that needed to be addressed.

Focus on strengths

Depending on the number of family members involved, and the extent to which they talk, the problem identification may take up much of the second session. The lists of problems and the talk about problems can seem rather negative. In the words of one family member involved in Collaborative Family Work: 'It looks like we are hopeless, doesn't it?' It is important to explain to family members that it is normal to have problems and that everyone has them, and that the listing of problems does not mean that the family is hopeless. In fact, family members being able to talk openly about problems can be considered a feature of a well-functioning family.

Nevertheless, identifying family strengths as part of, or following, the problem identification can help to develop an optimistic and hopeful atmosphere in the sessions. It can also help to make the problem lists less overwhelming for family members. Each family member might therefore be asked during the problem-identification stage to identify at least one thing that they like about the other family members, or one thing they enjoy doing with other family members, or one incident when another family member was kind or helpful towards them. These strengths can then be written down in the same way as the problems were written down. The lists might therefore include strengths along with the issues or problems identified.

Case study: Problem identification

Worker:	Now I explained to you before, Rebekah and Ilana, about the process we are going to go through starting with the problem identification.
Rebekah:	You're going to get us to talk about our problems.
Worker:	I am going to ask you to talk about your problems—that's the first step, and then we look at what you want to achieve, what your aims are and then what we can do to achieve the aims.
Ilana:	So you have got two hours to talk about all these problems?
Worker:	Today I can stay for an hour or a little bit longer if necessary.
Ilana:	Okay.
Worker:	I think you will be very worn out by the time an hour is up.
Rebekah:	Alright.
Worker:	I would like you to tell me the things that are worrying you—that are upsetting you, that you want to change. You have already talked about a few things, Rebekah—about seeing your dad, for example—but I want you to have a go, Rebekah, and your mum, at making a list of all the things that worry you and once we have worked them out we want to see which one we would like to work on first.
Ilana:	Isn't the whole reason why we are here to fix her up (referring to Rebekah)?
Rebekah:	And you.
Worker:	It's to sort out the problems between you. It

	is based on the idea that no one is wrong or at fault—just that there are some problems between you.
Ilana:	But there wouldn't be any problems between us if she listened to me and did what she's told—simple.
Worker:	The way this works is there may be problems between you—let's try and work out what they are.
Ilana:	Okay.
Worker:	So can we start with you, Rebekah? Do you want to tell me all the things that worry you, Rebekah—the things that you would like to improve?
Rebekah:	That my mum would stop yelling at me.
Ilana:	If you did what you were told to do I wouldn't yell.
Worker:	I am going to write that down, Rebekah. This is your list—first you want your mum to stop yelling.
Rebekah:	Yes, and I would like the kids to stop teasing me at school.
Worker:	Okay.
Rebekah:	And the teachers to stop giving me detention and everything like that.
Ilana:	Well stop getting into fights and they won't give you detention—that's easy.
Worker:	So we have—you want your mum to stop yelling, you want the kids to stop teasing you, what was the next one?
Rebekah:	I want to see my dad.
Worker:	Was there another one you said that I missed?
Ilana:	Yes, she thinks that the teachers are picking on her.

Worker:	Teachers to stop picking on you.
Ilana:	I think she should have detention if she gets into fights at school and stuff.
Worker:	Well—what we want to do now is just get our list. This is what we have so far, Rebekah (showing the list to Rebekah)—what else? Tell me about your friends, do you have any friends at school?
Rebekah:	I have one friend. I hang out with her when I don't go to school.
Worker:	Does she go to school?
Rebekah:	No.
Ilana:	Tell him the truth—you said you were going to be honest to him.
Worker:	How old is she?
Rebekah:	She's 16.
Worker:	And when you don't go to school, you go out with her?
Rebekah:	Yes, we go the mall and the supermarket and everything.
Ilana:	So can I ask you, do you think it is okay for an 11-year-old to hang out with a 16-year-old down the shopping centre?
Worker:	No, I don't think it's okay, and the school doesn't think it's okay either—do they, Rebekah? Do you like doing that?
Rebekah:	Yeah, it's fun. I like it way better than going to school. School's not fun when you get teased and the teachers pick on you and everything.
Worker:	Yes, okay. I understand that and we have got that down—that the kids are teasing you at school and the teachers are picking on you and they are things that worry you.
Rebekah:	Yep.
Worker:	Do you have any other friends at school?

Rebekah:	Nope.
Worker:	No, okay. What about other things you would like to change?
Ilana:	I would like her to do more things around the house.
Worker:	So your mum yelling at you—is that about doing things around the house?
Rebekah:	No.
Ilana:	It's about everything—you have a really bad attitude.
Rebekah:	You do—you are the one that has a go at me.
Worker:	Well at the moment, Rebekah, I think you are doing really well because this is the first time you have been in a meeting like this.
Ilana:	This is the best she has been forever.
Worker:	You are doing well, Rebekah.
Ilana:	I want to see what she's like when you leave— that will be interesting.
Worker:	Maybe we could come back to our rules we made up before—that we are not going to criticise each other.
Ilana:	Yeah, we will see.
Worker:	Okay, well we will come back and talk more about this, Rebekah. Now we will talk to your mum and get your mum to talk about her problems. Now tell me about your situation, Ilana.
Ilana:	And remember you are not allowed to interrupt, alright, because that's what she does. We get into arguments every night, because she doesn't want to go to bed, she does nothing when she gets home from school except sit in front of the TV.
Worker:	So you have arguments about this?
Rebekah:	You interrupt a lot.
Ilana:	Well I am the mum and I am meant to do

	things like that. You are meant to listen to me and do what I say.
Worker:	You have arguments about doing tasks and chores?
Ilana:	Yeah—she has three simple things: set the table, keep her room clean and make her bed and that's it. I don't think that is too much for an 11-year-old.
Worker:	So the arguments are about these three things—is this a problem for you, Rebekah, too?
Rebekah:	No.
Ilana:	Yeah, I think she enjoys the fights.
Worker:	What do you think about that, Rebekah?
Rebekah:	Well she starts them.
Ilana:	I don't—it's always you.
Rebekah:	It's always you.
Worker:	Do you like having the arguments, Rebekah?
Rebekah:	I don't really care.
Worker:	Okay, so we won't put that down as one of your problems but we have it down as one of your mum's.
Ilana:	Okay, what else . . . I don't like the fact she wags school.
Worker:	Okay.
Ilana:	Like, I get calls from the school nearly every second or third day saying 'Where is she? She's not at school.' and I have to take the calls at work and I get in trouble with my boss at work. She should just go to school.
Worker:	Okay, so we have got down the arguments— you don't like the arguments and you are worried about Rebekah not going to school.
Ilana:	I am worried about . . . she comes home with things like that bag from school and I don't know where she got it from.

Rebekah:	Well, my dad gives me money.
Ilana:	I don't know why he gives you money.
Worker:	So you're worried about what's she doing when she is not at school, is that right?
Ilana:	Yes.
Worker:	Anything else you would like to add?
Ilana:	I don't know.
Worker:	That's what we have got so far (showing the summary on a sheet of paper to Ilana and Rebekah).
Ilana:	Yeah, well I would just like her to listen to me and respect me a bit more. I would stop yelling if she just listened to me a bit more and respected me.
Worker:	So you would like Rebekah to listen?
Ilana:	Yes.
Worker:	I will put that on the list too—would you like your mum to listen to you more as well, Rebekah? Shall I put that on your list as well?
Rebekah:	Sure.
Worker:	Do you ever have any conversation between you that is positive—nice?
Ilana:	We used to.
Worker:	That sounds like a bit of a problem to me. Is that a problem for you, Rebekah? That you don't have any nice times with your mother? I will put that down for both of you—no good times together.
Worker:	Is that a problem for you, Ilana?
Ilana:	It would make my life a lot easier and we could do fun things because I am happy to take her out but I am not going to take her out and give her things if all she does is argue and yell at me.
Worker:	You would just like to get on better with Rebekah?

Ilana:	If we got on better maybe we would not have so many fights—I don't know.
Worker:	Was it always like this for you, Rebekah?
Ilana:	Don't lie.
Worker:	Say, two years ago—how was it, Ilana?
Ilana:	A couple of years ago it was really good. We used to always go out and do things. We would have fun on the weekend, she never missed school, she was doing really well at school, she had about four or five friends that came around the house and then all of a sudden she became this little person.
Rebekah:	That's because you yelled at me at the front of the school gates.
Ilana:	I can't remember doing it.
Worker:	You became upset about your mum embarrassing you at the school.
Rebekah:	Yes, and then everyone started teasing and then I did bad at work and then the teachers started teasing me.
Worker:	Does that still happen? Does your mum still go to the school and embarrass you or did it just happen once?
Rebekah:	Yes.
Worker:	So she still goes to the school? So that's another one we should add to the list?
Ilana:	So you want to walk to school? I can't see you walking to school, you would just nick off.
Worker:	I am putting this one on your list.
Ilana:	Well, if I could trust you to walk to school without nicking off down the shops, if I could go to work and not drop you off to school that would suit me.
Worker:	You are doing well at the moment, both of you, and you are participating in the process.

	I know this looks like an awful lot of problems.
Ilana:	Looks like we are hopeless.
Worker:	It looks like you have an awful lot of problems, but everyone has problems. There is nothing wrong with having problems. We just want to work out which are the most important ones and which ones we should start with. At the moment, we are just putting them on the table. Ilana, you were saying things were a lot better a couple of years ago—are there some good things you can tell me about Rebekah?
Ilana:	She has got a beautiful smile when she smiles.
Worker:	She has got a nice smile. I noticed before.
Ilana:	She used to be a real nice little kid who was always happy and would come home and tell me everything she did at school and all that stuff, and now she tells me nothing. She honestly comes home and sits on the lounge and tells me nothing.
Worker:	You used to do some nice things together and you would like those things to happen again?
Ilana:	That would be great—yes.
Worker:	You feel that she does have a lot to offer—she can be a nice daughter.
Ilana:	I think it's in there but I don't know what's going on in her mind. Certainly I know there is a really nice kid in there.
Worker:	So you feel Rebekah has a lot of potential?
Ilana:	She has got heaps of potential. When she puts her head down, she can do really well at school and she is really creative.
Worker:	We should put these things down as well— that she is creative and has a nice personality.

Ilana: I mean it's there—just she doesn't let me see
              it any more.
Worker: We don't want to talk about the problems
              and nothing else in these sessions—is there
              anything you can remember about having
              good times with your mum?
Rebekah: She used to give me stuff.
Worker: Okay.
Rebekah: And . . .
Ilana: I would give you stuff if you were good—why
              should I give you things if you don't behave?
Worker: So she used to give you stuff—was she nice to
              you, did she take you places?
Rebekah: Yeah.
Worker: Good—well, maybe we can talk about that
              a bit later. Let's look at where we are so far.
              All we are doing at the moment is finding out
              what the issues are and then we are going to
              start working out how to address them. We
              won't be able to solve all these problems
              but I have found if we start on one or two
              it can be helpful. Rebekah, you are worried
              about your mum's yelling, you are worried
              particularly about your mum going to school
              and yelling like she did, you're worried about
              the kids teasing you at school, about the fact
              you don't really have any good times with
              your mum and you're worried about the fact
              she won't let you see your dad.
Ilana: You're never going to see your dad.
Worker: You are also worried about the teachers at
              school not being nice to you and worried
              about your mum not listening to you.
Rebekah: Yes.
Worker: And Ilana, you are worried about the

arguments, about Rebekah not going to school, about what Rebekah does when she is not at school, and you're worried that she might be stealing.

Ilana: I have no idea what she's doing—she comes home with all these things . . . I don't know.

Worker: And you would like Rebekah to listen to you the same way that Rebekah wants you to listen to her, you are worried that you don't have the good times together like you used to, but you do feel that Rebekah is a creative person and has a nice personality and a bright future.

Ilana: I would love to take her to the pictures and that sort of stuff but why would I take her there when she will just be a smart arse?

Worker: So you would like a better relationship with her and you care about her a lot?

Ilana: I would love to—she is my daughter.

Worker: Do you feel like that too, Rebekah? You would like to have a better relationship with your mum?

Rebekah: Yep.

Ilana: That's what we get—'yep'.

Worker: Okay.

Rebekah's list
- Mum yelling
- Mum going to school
- The kids teasing at school
- No good times with Mum
- Mum won't let you see Dad
- Teachers not nice at school
- Mum doesn't listen
- Would like a better relationship with Mum

Ilana's list
- Too much arguing
- Concerned about Rebekah not going to school
- Worried about what Rebekah does when she is not at school
- Worried that she might be stealing
- Would like Rebekah to listen to her more
- No good times together any more
- Rebekah has a nice personality
- She is creative
- Want to have a relationship like before

The aim of this session was to help Ilana and Rebekah identify issues that were of concern to them, and that they might work on in the family sessions. The worker is focused on getting the list of the clients' problems and, consistent with the model, does not examine problems in depth at this stage. In order to deal with the potential negativity of listing problems, the worker includes some positives, and encourages Rebekah and her mother to talk about some good times they have had and some positives in their relationship. These positives are recorded along with the problems.

Ilana, despite agreeing to ground rules in the earlier session, continually makes negative remarks about and to Rebekah. On only one occasion does the worker remind Ilana of the ground rules, and then it is in a rather gentle manner. The rationale for this is that the worker does not wish to be seen as the enforcer of ground rules and feels that the session is progressing well despite the mother's comments. In fact, the mother comments that she has not known Rebekah to be so good. The aim of the session is to facilitate a discussion about the issues facing mother and daughter, and to identify some positives in their lives. In the process, mother and daughter begin to communicate in a way that they do not usually do.

The problem lists are written down as far as possible in the words of the family members. The problems are listed in terms of their concerns and worries rather than using blaming language. The positive issues on the list also help to modify the potential for the list to appear blaming.

Chapter summary

This chapter continued the description of the steps in the Collaborative Family Work model. It discussed reviewing the previous session and moving on to problem identification. It outlined the procedure for identifying issues as the family members see them and it discussed some for the issues faced by workers: What if clients don't identify the real issues? What does focusing on the here and now mean? How do you incorporate strengths? The next chapter considers what should be worked on first and setting goals.

6
Deciding what to work on first and setting goals

The next step is for the workers and the family members to decide which problem or problems to work on first. In most cases, it is appropriate to start with one common problem—for example, the arguments that occur between family members or the inability to agree on whether a young person should leave school. On other occasions, it may be appropriate to work on more than one problem.

Principles for deciding on problems
In making the decision about which problem or problems to work on first, the following principles can be followed.

The problem is a genuine problem for the family members
As far as possible, all family members should feel they are working on issues of concern to them. If the problem to be worked on is not a genuine problem for all family members,

then it may be appropriate to work on more than one problem in each session. Sometimes a family member will agree to work on an issue identified by another family member on the understanding that the issue they have identified will also be addressed. For example, in the case of Rebekah and Ilana, Rebekah may only be prepared to work on the issue of her listening to her mother if her mother agrees to work on her wish to see her father on a regular basis. Each family member should have an opportunity for their genuine issues to be addressed.

The problem is solvable

It is best to start with problems that have a good chance of being resolved. Some immediate success at the beginning of the family work process provides an incentive to both worker and client. For example, it may not be appropriate to start with an issue relating to contact with an absent father if the father has consistently shown a lack of interest in having contact with the family. It is more likely to be a suitable issue to start with if the father has shown some interest in contact in the past. Similarly, it may not be appropriate to start with a problem relating to disagreement between a mother and her daughter in relation to her boyfriend if she is determined that she will keep seeing him whatever happens—whereas if the worker feels there may be some room for negotiation on both sides, it may a suitable issue with which to begin.

Similarly, if resources are available to help solve the problem, there is a greater chance of achieving short-term success. For example, if a young person raises the issue of returning to study, but there are no suitable institutions offering relevant and appropriate courses, then this would not be a good issue with which to start. On the other hand, if the young person has completed some schooling and there are suitable institutions available, then the wish to pursue further education might be a more 'solvable' issue.

The problem is related to the reason the client is a client

As discussed earlier, Collaborative Family Work is designed for work in the human services. Clients of human service agencies may be voluntary or involuntary; however, for the most part they are clients because of particular issues they face. These issues may relate, for example, to neglect of a child, criminal offending, truancy, illegal drug use or mental illness. In deciding which issues to work on, the reason the client is a client of the agency should be taken into account.

For example, if Collaborative Family Work is being offered to a young offender and their family, either by a probation officer or on referral from a juvenile justice agency, then factors relating to the young person's offending will be relevant to deciding which issue to address first. If, for example, a young man is required to attend for drug treatment and is having difficulty doing so, then this issue might take precedence. The family members might discuss ways in which the attendance at drug treatment can be facilitated. To take another example, a young person and their family might be involved in Collaborative Family Work because of disruptive behaviour at school, and there may be a strong possibility of the young person being excluded from school unless this behaviour improves. In this instance, addressing the issue of school behaviour is likely to be a priority.

The Collaborative Family Work model emphasises the importance of family members deciding what their problems are and what problems need to be addressed. Yet I am suggesting that certain issues should take precedence because of the legal issues involved—for example, the young person's attendance for drug treatment or the young person's disruptive behaviour in school. In these cases, it is up to the skill of the workers and their powers of persuasion to encourage the family members to focus on particular issues. The overriding principle of the Collaborative Family Work model is, however, that the family members must agree that the problems they work on are problems for *them*.

As discussed earlier, there may be good reasons why family members wish to work on issues that may seem peripheral to the worker. Sometimes issues are too personal to deal with in the early meetings. Sometimes the family members wish to begin work on issues that are not threatening until they begin to trust that the workers can actually help them. Sometimes presenting problems are best approached through other issues—for example, much of the work done with this model has been done with young offenders and their families; however, the workers report that offending is rarely raised in the sessions. Yet often the work on family communication issues leads to reduced offending.

Ethical values

The worker should also encourage the family members to work on issues that are consistent with pro-social or ethical values. For example, a man involved in Collaborative Family Work may have a problem with what he perceives as his partner's lack of support. He may want his partner to carry out more tasks around the home and generally be more supportive of him. The worker may feel that working on such a problem would be supporting a patriarchal view on the client's part. In this instance, the worker would discourage the family members from working on this problem.

Practical 'here and now' problems

As mentioned in the discussion about problem identification, the focus of Collaborative Family Work is on practical and current issues rather than past hurts or experiences. In deciding which issues to address, this principle is again important. See Figure 6.1 for guidelines for deciding which issues to work on.

Figure 6.1 Deciding which issues to work on

> - It is a genuine problem for members of the family.
> - The problem is solvable.
> - The problem is related to the reason the client is a client—for example, truancy or a court order.
> - It is ethical.
> - Practical 'here and now' problems get priority.

Developing goals

Once a decision has been made to work on one or two problems, the next step is to set goals. A goal is a specific written statement that identifies what family members would like to achieve in relation to a specific problem and when they wish to achieve it. It is a statement about what the family members want to happen. Figure 6.2 outlines the principles involved in developing goals.

Goals are an essential component of problem-solving interventions and of many family therapy approaches. Goals are important for several reasons. A number of studies and reviews of studies in the human services have found that when workers and clients agree on specific goals, outcomes are likely to be better than in situations when no goals have been set (Smokowski & Wodarski 1996; Trotter 2004, 2006). Goals provide a sense of direction for family members, and provide something to work towards. The process of developing and agreeing on goals within family work sessions also helps to develop family communication and provides family members with an opportunity to work together on tasks that are non-threatening. Goals also provide a method by which family members and workers can assess the progress of the intervention.

In developing goals, each family member should be asked what they wish to achieve in relation to the problem. For example, in a family session involving a couple, Jacob and Evie, and their three children, Jacob identified a problem with Evie spending a lot of time with her elderly mother and her disabled brother. He was unemployed and he felt that she should spend more time with him, whereas she felt that it was important for her to support her mother and brother. This issue caused friction between the couple, which also impacted on the children. It was a problem for Jacob as he wanted to spend more time with his wife and it was a problem for Evie because she felt that she had a responsibility to her mother and that Jacob should understand this. It was also a problem for the children, as it created family conflict.

The worker discussed this issue with the couple and the children, the oldest of whom, at the age of 16, made an important contribution to the discussion. It was agreed that the goal was to reach agreement between Jacob and Evie regarding the amount of time she should spend with her mother and brother. They both felt that this was urgent, and that they would like the goal to be achieved within two weeks. The goal was therefore written down as:

Within two weeks to reach agreement between Jacob and Evie regarding the amount of time she spends with her mother and brother.

Goals often involve reaching agreement on a particular issue such as this. To take another example, a mother, Maria, and her 17-year-old son, Kevin, were experiencing a lot of friction around his staying in bed until two or three o'clock in the afternoon. Maria wanted him to get up earlier and do something productive, even if he did not go to work or school. Kevin just wanted his mother to leave him alone to make his own decisions about how he lived his life. Maria and Kevin and the worker agreed on a goal:

For Maria and Kevin to reach agreement this week regarding when Kevin should get out of bed.

Figure 6.2: Principles for developing goals

- **Goals should be achievable.** Collaborative Family Work is a strengths-based model, which relies on achieving small successes along the way rather that setting out to solve big problems that are difficult to solve. For example, it is easier to achieve a goal of having some regular positive conversations between family members than it is to achieve a goal of having no family arguments. The worker, in particular, must be confident that the goal can be achieved. If the worker feels that a goal is too ambitious, then it is best to break the goal down into small, achievable parts.
- **Goals should be agreed to by all family members.** Like decisions about which problems to work on, it is best if all family members agree on the goal. For the most part, if problems revolve around an issue that is common to all family members, then common goals can be set.

Sometimes, however, family members have different goals. For example, Rebekah's goal might be to have contact with her father on a regular basis and her mother Ilana's goal might be for Rebekah to not see her father at all. In this instance, it is a matter of rewording the goal so that both parties can agree to it. The goal becomes: 'To reach agreement about how often Rebekah sees her father'.

- **Goals should be measurable.** It should be possible for the worker and each family member to know whether or not a goal has been achieved. For this to occur, the goal needs to have a timeline and to be stated in sufficiently specific terms so that the worker and family members know whether it has been carried out.

- **Goals may be long or short term.** For example, the goal 'To improve communication between family members' may be a long-term goal. It may refer to family members talking to each other in a civil and responsive manner on a regular basis as part of a regular pattern of interaction—in other words, for the family to develop a new way of interacting for the long term. Long-term goals of this nature are very difficult to measure, partly because they are not time-limited and partly because they are not defined sufficiently clearly for workers and family members to know whether they have been carried out. Nevertheless, they do have a place in the Collaborative Family Work model. They can help family members to identify a sense of direction for the long term. The goals to obtain a university degree, to leave home, to get married, to buy a house or to have children are important long-term goals that can be and are expressed in family work sessions. These can be described, however, as general life goals that may set the context for the more specific goals commonly used in Collaborative Family Work.

Specific short–term measurable goals are commonly used in Collaborative Family Work. These are the goals that have been discussed so far in this chapter. Specific short–term goals that can be achieved within the six to ten weeks of the family work intervention provide the basis on which tasks and strategies can be developed. They often represent small steps towards longer-term goals.

Goals and tasks

There are times when goals and tasks can become confused. For example, in one family the family members said they argued all the time and rarely had civil conversations with each other. They indicated that they would like the arguments to stop and they would like to be able to get on together like a 'normal family'. In helping the family members to develop a goal in relation to arguments, the worker helped the family members to determine what exactly they were seeking. Did they want to never argue at all? What level and frequency of arguments would they be satisfied with? What does it mean to get on together like a normal family? How often did they wish to have normal civil conversations?

The worker and the family members discussed this, and at first said the goal was for the arguments to stop. The worker asked what this meant, and they said they would not mind having occasional arguments but not all the time. The worker then asked whether it would be better to focus on developing some positive conversations rather than simply stopping arguments. The family members agreed to this, and eventually came up with a goal:

> For the family members to have regular positive conversations at least twice a day when each person is civil to each other and talks to each other without raised voices and listens to what others have to say. This is to be achieved within two weeks.

The workers (in this example, there were two workers) then became confused. Was the goal to reduce family conflict and the task to have two conversations each week where each person listened to the others without raised voices? Or was the goal to have these conversations and the next step to set tasks such as meeting at a certain time to have the conversation? It is important to be clear about the difference between the goal—what you want to achieve—and the task—how you will achieve it. There is, however, an inevitable degree of overlap between some goals and tasks. The use of rating scales to assist in developing goals also helps to make general goals more specific and thus to avoid this confusion.

Goals should be:

- Agreed to by family members
- Achievable
- Measurable
- Time-limited

Rating scales and goals

Rating scales were discussed in Chapter 3. The use of the problem rating scale can help to define problems and goals and help to decide the extent to which a goal has been achieved. For example, family members might rate the current state of family communication with an average rating of 2 on a five-point scale—'the problem is very serious but you are able to cope with most everyday tasks'. The family members can then be asked to describe what the rating of 2 means in more detail. They might say, for example, that two family members rarely speak positively and this creates friction in the family.

The family members can then be asked what they would like the rating to be or what they think they might be able to achieve. They might say 4—'The problem is not that serious and you are able to cope with it reasonably'. They can then be asked to describe how it might look if the problem were rated at 4. They might say that the arguments between the family members would have stopped and the family members would talk to each other in a friendly way most of the time and that other family members would feel that the house was a more enjoyable place to be in. The goal could then be specified:

> The goal is to improve the rating of family communication from 2 to 4 within the next four weeks. This means that Tristan and Seville will talk to each other in a friendly way at least occasionally (once per day) and that they will argue in front of other family members in a way that upsets them no more than twice per week.

There may be families where this level of detail in the expression of goals is difficult to achieve; however, it is important that the family members and the workers understand as much as possible what it is that they are trying to achieve and when they expect to achieve it.

What if goals are not achieved?

There will often be occasions when goals are set by family members and, despite the best efforts of the workers and family members to ensure that the goals are realistic and achievable, the goals may not be achieved. As emphasised throughout this book, Collaborative Family Work is a strengths-based model, and it is important that not achieving goals is not seen as a failure on the part of family members. If a goal is not achieved, then the goal is by definition a poorly constructed goal—as goals should be easily achievable. The goal can then be reviewed in terms of why it wasn't achieved. Was it too difficult? Was there insufficient family commitment to it? Did all family members agree to it? Was it clearly defined? Were the strategies put in place to achieve the goal not achieved or were they the wrong strategies?

Following this discussion, the goal can then either be abandoned, or reworked in such a way that it is likely to be achieved—or, alternatively, the goal may be maintained but new strategies put in place to achieve the goal. This process is discussed further in the next chapter.

Case study: Deciding what to work on first and setting goals

Worker:	Hi, Rebekah. Hi, Ilana. Thanks very much for being here again today. What did you think about what we were talking about last week? How did you find it all?
Rebekah:	Yep, it was fine.
Worker:	Was it okay? There were a lot of problems we talked about. You didn't feel overwhelmed?
Ilana:	I think it was good that she was actually honest because some of the stuff I didn't know, so that was good.
Worker:	So some of the stuff you didn't know? Like . . . ?
Ilana:	Well, I didn't know the kids were teasing her that much at school.
Worker:	Oh, so you didn't realise how difficult things were for her?
Ilana:	Well, not really, because she just doesn't tell me anything. I just thought she was wagging just for the hell of it.

Worker:	So I suppose you wouldn't have heard about these things?
Ilana:	Not all of it, no.
Worker:	Because you hadn't been talking to each other? Was it like that for you too, Rebekah? That you hadn't heard what your mum thought?
Rebekah:	Some of it I had. But the rest, no.
Worker:	I suppose it's good to actually have a conversation when you're not yelling at each other.
Ilana:	Yeah! That was one of the things I was surprised about, that we didn't yell at each other that much. So maybe having that third person in the room calms her down or something.
Worker:	Well I'm really pleased at how you both participated. And I'm sure doing this can be very helpful.
Ilana:	Yeah, well let's see if she's that good again today.
Worker:	Yeah, okay. So the next step—last week we talked about working through the things that worry you and we developed the lists of all your problems. I have them here. You can change that list any time you want if there are other problems you want to put on it. If at any time you want to add other things, just speak up. But what we want to do now is work out where we are going to start. Which of the problems we talked about would be best for us to start with?
Ilana:	Well, it's easy—she just has to listen to me.
Worker:	So the thing that worries you the most is that she doesn't . . .

Ilana:	Yeah, well if she listened to me, then hopefully she'd understand a bit more about what's going on.
Rebekah:	Yeah, well if she let me go see my dad more often then I'd be nicer. But she just doesn't let me.
Ilana:	Why do you want to go see him? Why? Because he bribes you with money?
Rebekah:	No.
Ilana:	Well then why do you want to see him?
Rebekah:	Because he's my dad!
Worker:	So, you're saying (talking to Rebekah) that the thing you're most worried about is, as far as your mum's concerned, the fact that she won't let you see your dad?
Rebekah:	Yep.
Worker:	And you want to be able to see your dad? I'm going to write that down—that what you want to work on is that you want to see your dad.
Ilana:	I want to know why you want to see your dad when he didn't want to see you for years. You didn't care about it for six years and now, all of a sudden, because he's giving you money . . .
Worker:	Okay then, well let's say the main thing Rebekah wants is to see her dad and the main thing you want is for Rebekah to . . .
Ilana:	Well, why should I let her see her dad? He's never gone to the courts, he doesn't care about her. Why should I let her see him?
Worker:	Okay, then we can explore all that—we can talk about that and work out what we can do about it. But your thing is about listening and Rebekah not listening to you and not being nice to you.

Ilana:	She doesn't—I mean, I'm saying something and she just starts arguing with me, about everything, so . . .
Worker:	So, Rebekah, we've got that you want to see your dad, and your mum wants you to listen to her. So when you say you want to see your dad, Rebekah, let's just talk a bit about what this means. When you say you want to see your dad, do you mean you want to see him every week or every month or every day or what? What actually do you want?
Ilana:	Let me guess. You want to see him every day because he gives you money.
Rebekah:	No, every second day.
Worker:	How far away does he live from you?
Rebekah:	Not far. I just catch the bus usually.
Ilana:	He lives two suburbs away and I'm not going to take her there. I'm not going to drive her two suburbs away. I'm too busy.
Rebekah:	That's why I catch the bus.
Worker:	You can catch the bus and that's okay—is it in the daytime?
Ilana:	Look, she used to catch the bus. And he wouldn't be there when she got there. She's 11 years old and you were doing this when you were, what, 9 years old—going to your dad's. And we'd set up the time and he'd never be there so she'd sit there for an hour on her own in a bad neighbourhood and then she'd have to catch the bus back home.
Worker:	Okay, so we just want to work out for the moment what Rebekah wants. I'm listening to what you are saying, Ilana, and I understand the problem, but let's just see . . . how often do you see your dad now?

Rebekah:	Twice a month.
Ilana:	When?
Worker:	That's because you go on your own when your mum doesn't know?
Rebekah:	Yeah! Because she won't let me.
Worker:	And is he there? When you go on the bus, is he there?
Rebekah:	Yeah.
Ilana:	So . . . what, he's been there every time you've turned up?
Rebekah:	Mmm hmm (nodding).
Worker:	So we're going to say, you'd like to see your dad—you're saying every second day. That's what your aim is, that's your goal, isn't it?
Rebekah:	Mmm hmm (nodding).
Ilana:	So how's she going to do that? She's got school five days a week. How are you going to see your dad every second day when you've got school, homework, chores?
Worker:	So we're going to write that down. That's what you'd like, you'd like to see your dad three or four times a week. So that's her goal, Ilana, it doesn't have to happen. We're just asking Rebekah what she'd like and this is her main thing and that's what she'd like.
Ilana:	You can have it as a goal but I don't know whether you'll get it. We'll see.
Worker:	Well, we can talk about how we're going to deal with it. You're saying, Ilana, that you want Rebekah to be nicer to you, to listen to you. Can you talk a bit more about that? What do you want from Rebekah? What would you like?
Ilana:	I'd like her to listen to me when I ask her to, like, set the table for me. And I explained to

	her that I've worked all day. I come home and I cook the dinner. All she has to do is set the table and sit down and eat dinner. But, no she yells at me.
Rebekah:	But you can still do that, it's not like you don't have a few minutes . . .
Ilana:	But why should I do everything? You're 11 years old—you can help me out a little bit.
Worker:	Because you're working and you don't have a lot of time.
Ilana:	Yeah. I work, and I cut my hours back so that I could pick her up from school. So that I know that she's coming home straight after school instead of going God-knows-where.
Worker:	Okay.
Ilana:	And the least she could do is do that. And I try and explain to her why I want things done, but she doesn't listen to me. So then she just gets angry with me and does whatever she wants to do and sits in front of the telly and watches crap.
Worker:	So your aim is for when you talk to Rebekah, that she'll listen to you and . . . not yell back at you but also do some of the . . .
Ilana:	Yeah, well even if she just listens and if she doesn't understand why I'm saying things, just tell me. 'Look, Mum, I don't understand what you're asking or I don't know why you want me to do that or . . . ' But she doesn't—she just argues.
Worker:	So if you're asking her to do something, you want her to just listen to you and talk to you?
Ilana:	Yeah.
Worker:	And not . . .
Ilana:	If she doesn't want to do it then she needs to

	tell me why she doesn't want to do it, instead of just going off the handle and . . .
Worker:	Okay, so your aim is simply for Rebekah to listen to you and talk to you, particularly when you're asking her to do things.
Ilana:	Yes.
Worker:	And you also want her to help you with things around the house?
Ilana:	Yes.
Worker:	We've got two different problems here.
Ilana:	Yeah, that's not surprising.
Worker:	Rebekah, you've got a problem with your dad and Ilana, you've got a problem with listening and helping around the house. And we need to sort out how we can deal with these two different problems. So I think the first thing we're going to do is just explore a bit more. Talk a bit more about the two things and about what's been happening. And what you've tried and what's worked and what hasn't worked.

Goals for Rebekah
- To see her father every second day

Goals for Ilana
- For Rebekah to listen to her and talk to her, particularly when she is asked to do things
- For Rebekah to help with things around the house

In this transcript, the worker reviews the previous week, particularly in terms of how Rebekah and Ilana found the session. The worker focuses on the positives that came from the previous week's discussion—they participated well in the session and they understood more about each other. In discussing the goals, the worker does not use the rating scales, but instead attempts to define the goals as specifically as possible. However, the goals as they were written down still need further definition, including when they should be achieved. This can be done following the problem exploration, which is the next stage in the model.

Chapter summary

In deciding what to work on first, it has been argued that workers and family members should focus on issues which are solvable, ethical, related to the reason the client is a client and practical. Similarly, in the development of goals it is important that they are achievable, measurable and agreed to by all family members. The overlap between long- and short-term goals, and goals and strategies, can lead to some confusion for workers and family members. The model works best however when workers help family members to be as clear as possible about what they want to achieve.

7

Problem exploration and developing strategies

This chapter discusses problem exploration and developing strategies to address problems and goals. It is the longest chapter because it outlines in some detail the actual strategies that have been used by workers who have used the model in human services settings. It is also a long chapter because problem exploration and developing strategies are interrelated, so need to be dealt with together.

Exploring problems

There is often debate among those who use the Collaborative Family Work model about when the problem exploration should occur. Some say that goal-setting can't be successful if the workers and family members have not explored the problem in some detail. For example, if family interaction has been characterised by constant arguments for many years, then a goal of eliminating arguments altogether might be unrealistic, whereas if the arguments have only been going on for a few weeks, then the goal of elimination of the arguments might be reasonable. If the arguments involve physical fighting, this might also influence the nature of the goals.

On the other hand, knowing what the family members want is an important part of defining the problem and providing direction to the work. The process of exploring the problem involves identifying what has been tried before, what has worked and what hasn't. This can be difficult to do if the family members are unclear about what they are seeking.

It is therefore recommended that some problem exploration occurs during the initial process of identifying problems. Goals can then be discussed and defined following the decision about which problems to work on. The more detailed problem exploration can then follow the setting of the goals. The goals can be revised following the problem exploration if necessary.

As emphasised throughout this book, Collaborative Family Work is a dynamic model that is designed to be used flexibly and in response to the changing nature of problems and of the way families define their problems. At any stage in the process, including the problem exploration, both the problem and the goal may be redefined.

The aim of the problem exploration stage is to find out more about the problem. Some questions that can be asked to facilitate this process include:

- *When did the problem begin?* Has the family had this problem for many years, or is it a more recent issue? Has it developed gradually or suddenly? If, for example, the problem is one of continual arguing, did it start with small arguments between one or two family members or has it always been there?

- *What is the nature of the problem?* Does the arguing take place between all family members or just some? How do those not directly involved react and do they get involved? Do the arguments involve abusive behaviour on the part of any family member, either physically or verbally? Are there victims and perpetrators in the arguments? What are the arguments about? Do they focus on the same issue or are they focused on a range of issues? What are the issues?

- *What efforts have been made to solve the problem?* Have individual family members done anything to try to stop the arguing? Have they tried to discuss the situation with each other? Have they told each other about how they feel about the arguments? Has anyone tried to mediate in any way between those family members most directly involved? Has anyone tried specific strategies like leaving the house, not responding or yelling back?

- *What has been successful and what has been unsuccessful?* Have some of the attempted methods of solving the problem actually had an impact? If, for example, one family member attempted to make peace between two family members, did this help or hinder the situation? Was this done more than once, and did it work better on some occasions than others?

- *Have there been occasions when the problem was not there?* If there have been times when there was no arguing going on, why was this? What was different about those occasions compared with the usual situation when arguing occurs? Was someone not present?

Was it at the time of a special event? What was it like when the problem wasn't there? Were people happier? What were they doing? Who was talking to whom? What was different about those occasions?

- *Are there particular obstacles preventing the solution of the problem?* For example, do one or two family members have problems with controlling anger? Is the problem simply that some family members have a 'short fuse' and they need to deal with this individually before the family issue can be addressed? Is one family member using mood-altering drugs or alcohol, which leads to arguments and violence regardless of what other family members do?

These questions are summarised in Figure 7.1.

Once the problem has been thoroughly explored, the family members and the workers may, as mentioned above, revise the problem definition and the goals. The next step is to begin discussing strategies to address the goals. However, developing strategies should not occur before the family members and the worker have agreed on what problem to work on and what they wish to achieve, or before a thorough examination of the problem and issues surrounding it has taken place. There is little point in pursuing solutions that have been tried before and failed, or pursuing solutions to a problem that is not clear. The challenge for the worker is to be clear about the problem and the goals, but at the same time to acknowledge that client definitions of problems change and the problems themselves change—sometimes from week to week and sometimes within sessions. The challenge for the worker is to provide order to the discussions, yet at the same time work to allow for the uncertainty and disorder that characterise most of the families who are likely to be involved in Collaborative Family Work.

Figure 7.1: Problem exploration

- When did the problem begin?
- What is the nature of the problem?
- What efforts have been made to solve it?
- What has been successful and what unsuccessful?
- Have there been occasions when the problem was not there? What was different about those occasions?
- Are there particular obstacles preventing solution of the problem?

Developing strategies and solutions

When the worker is satisfied that there is agreement on the problem definition and the goals, and the problem has been explored in sufficient detail, then the next step is to develop strategies to address the problem. A strategy or a task is any activity devised by the worker or family members to address a particular problem or to enhance family interaction. In some cases, workers using the model have preferred to use the term 'activities' rather than 'strategies' or 'tasks', as it is a more familiar term to many family members.

Strategies or activities may be undertaken in sessions or at home. There are several types of strategies. Facilitative strategies can be used in sessions or at home when the workers wish to set strategies that don't relate to specific problems. Problem-related strategies may be used in sessions to address specific problems or they may be developed in sessions to be undertaken at home by family members. Strategies may be carried out by family members or by the worker. Strategies may involve tasks that family members do together or they may involve individual family members doing tasks on their own.

In this chapter, strategies have been divided into session-based facilitative strategies, home-based facilitative strategies, problem-related session strategies and problem-related home strategies. In many cases, of course, these strategies overlap. Facilitative strategies that generally aim to improve family communication may be used as problem-related strategies if family communication is defined as a problem. Session strategies and home strategies are also often interrelated. For example, a listening skills or paraphrasing strategy, whereby family members practise listening to each other, may be carried out within a session. This task may then be continued at home—in other words, the session task is repeated as a home task.

Despite the overlap between the various strategies, it is important to make the distinction between types of strategies and for workers to understand what type of strategies they are using. Problem-related strategies should follow problem identification, prioritising, goals and exploration for the reasons explained earlier. Facilitative strategies do not necessarily follow these steps. Understanding these distinctions helps workers and families to know where they are in relation to the model at any given time. This is important to ensure that workers and families do not lose the sense of order and direction provided by the model.

The development of solutions or strategies should follow similar principles to the identification of problems and the development of goals. Figure 7.2 contains a checklist of the strategies listed below.

- Strategies should be specific and time-limited. Everyone involved should know what is to be done and when it is to be done by.

- Each family member should genuinely agree that the strategy is worthwhile and agree to carry it out.

- Strategies should be easily achieved. If a strategy is not carried out, it is because it has been poorly developed. The problem is with the strategy, not the person who did not carry it out.

- Strategies should be evenly distributed. Preferably, all family members should have some strategies or tasks to work on each week.

- There should not be too many strategies so as to overwhelm those carrying them out.

- Generally, they should relate directly to the problem that is being worked on and the goal that has been set in relation to the problem.

- Problem-related strategies (as opposed to facilitative strategies) should never be developed until the problems have been identified and goals set, and the problem has been explored. Setting strategies without having a clear understanding of the nature of the problem and what has been tried before runs the risk of repeating past failures and of putting into place solutions that may not address the problem.

- Strategies should be reasonable with regard to age, sex and socio-cultural variables. The process of ensuring that all family members understand and agree to the strategy will help to ensure that it does not breach any cultural sensitivities.

- Strategies should be oriented primarily towards increasing positive behaviours rather than decreasing negative ones. It is better to ask family members

to do something than to ask them to stop doing
something.

Figure 7.2: Strategies checklist

- Specific and time-limited
- Family members genuinely agree
- Easily achieved
- Evenly distributed
- Not too many
- Relate directly to the problem
- Or can be generally facilitative
- Reasonable with regard to age, sex and culture
- Positive

Facilitative strategies

Facilitative strategies are general strategies that don't focus
on particular problems or goals. While facilitative strategies
may be carried out at home, they are most commonly used
in sessions to increase family communication or simply to
provide workers with helpful activities when they are unsure
about what to do next. Facilitative strategies can be used to
inject some positive feelings into the family work, particularly if the worker senses that discussion about problems is
becoming negative and overwhelming for family members.
Facilitative strategies can be particularly useful in the early
stages of family work when the focus is on problem definition and goal-setting. They can also be useful towards the
end of the early sessions so that the family members have
something to do between sessions, even though problems
may not have been defined or goals set. There are many
examples of facilitative strategies, some of which are discussed below.

Family members might describe what they like about each other. This is one of the most commonly used strategies. Workers are sometimes apprehensive about using this strategy because they feel that the family members will not respond appropriately or will not be able to think of things they like about each other. However, my practical experience suggests that this is not the case. The fact that family members have chosen to be involved indicates that there is at least some degree of connection between family members, and that they have some positive feelings towards each other. Also, if the family members have been prepared for the work as discussed earlier, and if they have been involved in developing ground rules, this should have helped them to develop a positive orientation towards each other and towards using strategies like this.

One method of helping family members to identify what they like (or respect) about each other is through the use of strengths cards (St Lukes Innovative Resources 2008). These cards contain words such as 'friendly', 'committed', 'caring', 'capable', 'enthusiastic', 'understanding' and 'adventurous', and can be shown to family members who then can use them to identify each other's strengths. The family members can be given the cards by other family members as they decide.

Another facilitative strategy or activity that can be used in sessions involves identifying times when family members have been able to get on well, including particular activities that they have enjoyed. Family members might talk about a family holiday, how they enjoy going to the movies together or how they like to sit down as a family and watch a particular television show.

Teaching family members listening skills is another facilitative strategy. The worker may feel that family members talk over each other or do not hear what is said to them. The family members can be asked whether they would like to participate in a listening exercise. One family member can be asked to speak about something of interest to them and the other family members can be asked to summarise what has been said. The family member who spoke first can then provide feedback to the other family members regarding the accuracy of their listening.

Listening can be a difficult process for people who are not used to it, and family members may need some guidance for this strategy to work well. The period of speaking might need to be limited to one or two minutes. The family members who are listening can be encouraged to clear their minds of any other thoughts and focus on what the other person is saying. They can be encouraged to ask questions if they are unsure of the meaning of what is being said, and to refrain from making any other comments other than to repeat some of the things that have been said to check that they understand correctly. When this strategy is first undertaken, it may be advantageous for the speaker to talk about an issue that is not controversial and is unlikely to raise the emotional level of other family members. It might, for example, be appropriate for the person speaking to talk about something that happened in a TV show so that the family members can begin to understand the process with a non-threatening example.

In the process of helping family members to improve their listening skills, they can also be encouraged to use non-blaming language. In many cases, family members involved in Collaborative Family Work have developed habits of blaming each other for difficulties that arise. Family members can be encouraged to use 'I' statements that reflect how they feel rather than statements that blame others. If, for example, a father says about his son, Omar:

> He lost that job because he stayed out so late at night drinking and couldn't get up in the morning—he is just irresponsible.

The worker can help the father to say this in non-blaming terms—for example:

> Omar has shown that he can get jobs and can work well although he lost his last job because he was late too often. This is something he could work on.

In one example of a facilitative session-based strategy, the workers and the family members decided to develop a strengths sheet. The mother and son involved in the session, Marija and Christopher, brainstormed what they felt were each other's strengths and their own strengths, and the workers wrote this down (see Figure 7.3). At the following session, the workers brought along the strengths sheets to be displayed and reviewed. The workers felt this was very effective because Christopher and Marija had not identified these things before. Their usual communication was characterised only by negative comments.

Facilitative home-based strategies

Facilitative strategies can also be carried out at home. Some examples are provided below. Family members can be asked to reflect on the ground rules that have been developed in the session and try to think of any other ground rules which they might discuss in the next session. A discussion about

Figure 7.3: Christopher's and Marija's strengths sheets

Marija's strengths

Marija identified her strengths as:
- Thoughtful
- Generous
- Loving
- Fair
- Honest
- Happy
- Kind
- Protective

Christopher indentified Marija's strengths as:
- Good at taking care of me
- Loving
- Capable

Christopher's strengths

Christopher identified his strengths as:
- Understanding
- Friendly
- Humble
- Practical
- Helpful
- Contented
- Reliable
- Careful
- Responsible

Marija indentified Christopher's strengths as:
- Willingness to do anything asked of him
- Kind
- Gentle
- Very loyal

these can then be held at the beginning of the next session. Similarly, between sessions, family members can be asked to identify issues that they would like to add to their problem lists. These can include problems that they might not have remembered during the session or strengths of their own or other family members. These can then be added to the list of issues at the next session.

Another popular facilitative home task is for family members to participate in an activity that they enjoy, and that does not involve family conflict. This strategy can be discussed in the session and a suitable activity then carried out between sessions. This might involve watching a television program together, going fishing, sharing a meal at home, going out for dinner, playing a game of football or chess, planting a veggie garden, or any other activity that family members might enjoy.

If a listening skills session strategy has been used, it is often appropriate to follow this strategy up at home. In one example, the family practised listening skills, and paraphrasing and responding to emotional content, in a family work session. They then followed this up at home. However, for the home strategy they selected an issue that was not too difficult: what TV program they would watch on the only TV in the house. Each person talked about one program that they would like to watch each week and the other family members listened using the reflective listening skills they had practised in the Collaborative Family Work session. The family members reported back that the strategy had caused much laughter but had been carried out successfully.

Problem-based home strategies

There are many strategies available to address problems and goals. In fact, if the variety of problems and goals in families is unlimited, then so are the strategies to deal with them. Outlined below are some examples of home-based strategies that have been used in Collaborative Family Work.

Samantha and her partner, Bill, have frequent arguments over the fact that Samantha is rarely home. Samantha's three children, aged 14, 10 and 6, are cared for most of the time by Bill, who has no children of his own. The three children often become involved in the arguments between Bill and Samantha, and they don't like the fact that they see so little of their mother.

Samantha has a mental illness and is on regular medication. She spends most of her days caring for her sister's five children, who have been placed in the care of her elderly mother by the Child Protection Department. Samantha is worried that Child Protection will take the children if she does not look after them. In discussion with the family and the worker in the family work sessions, she said that she feels burdened by the responsibility but feels that she must support her mother and sister. Her goal and that of the family was for her to spend more time with her own family but at the same time to feel comfortable that her sister's children were being cared for. The family agreed on a number of strategies.

The first strategy was for Samantha to talk to her mother and her sister about her need to have more contact with her own family and discuss whether there were some alternative arrangements that could be made to care for the five children at least on some days of the week. The strategy was simply to discuss this and to see whether the family could come up with possible options. Another strategy agreed to by the family was for Samantha to explain to her mother and sister that she could not always look after the children if she was given very short notice—that it was fine for her mother to ask her if she could mind the children, but there would be times when something else had been arranged when she would be unable to do so. There would be times when her own family commitments would have to take precedence. These strategies were written down so that they were clear, and Samantha was to report back on their implementation the following week.

While the family members involved in the Collaborative Family Work session were enthusiastic about helping Samantha to address the issue of the time she had for her own family, they were reluctant to produce strategies for themselves. The worker encouraged them to do so, following the principle that as far as possible strategies should be shared between family members. A strategy was therefore developed for Bill. This was to identify the times during the week when he would like Samantha to spend time with him and the children. Bill was to do this with the children and let Samantha know the most suitable times before she had the discussion with her mother.

Here is another example of a home-based strategy.

A 13-year-old boy, Simon, attended Collaborative Family Work with his father following a referral from

Child Protection. Simon had been reported to Child Protection because he had run away from home and had told a youth worker that he could not go home again as his father had hit him. Nevertheless, Child Protection had returned him to the care of his father.

One of the problems identified by Simon in the sessions was that his father did not have enough time for him and did not do enough things with him. Simon was asked to suggest a strategy to address this, and he said he would like to play chess with his father—something they used to do years ago. His father agreed, and they played chess the following week. The chess games subsequently continued each week, often two or three times a week, and they proved to be a very helpful strategy in restoring the relationship between Simon and his father—so much so that some weeks after the family work finished, the father wrote to the worker to say how well they were getting on and that they were continuing to play chess on a regular basis.

Often, strategies involve 'quid pro quo'—you do something for me and I will do something for you.

A 13-year-old girl, Jemima, was referred by a court to Collaborative Family Work after she admitted to stealing a car. In discussing the issues with her mother, who attended the Collaborative Family Work session with her, she said that she did not like school, found homework a waste of time and was always late for school. Her mother talked about Jemima's problems with school but her biggest concern was that she went to bed very late—usually after midnight—because she sat on her computer until that time. She was then unable to get up in the morning and was constantly late for school. This was more of a problem because her younger sister liked to walk to school with her and she often waited for her and was also late for school.

Following some exploration of the issues, it became apparent that Jemima could not get access to the computer until about 10.30 or 11.00 at night because her mother had arranged for her younger sister to use the computer until then so she could do her homework. Jemima and her mother then agreed that Jemima could have the computer from 9.00 until 10.30 p.m. Jemima's sister could only use the computer until 9.00 p.m. In return, Jemima agreed that she would get off the computer at 10.30 p.m. and would get out of bed the next day by 8.00 a.m., which was early enough to get to school on time. This strategy was agreed on in the session. It was then carried out the following week, reviewed in the next session and put in place as a regular pattern.

Another example of a 'quid pro quo' problem-based home task related to the Pratt family.

During the week, 17-year-old Sol would stay with his father but at the weekend he would stay with his mother and his sister. He liked to go to bed late and sleep most of the day, and would become abusive to his mother and sister if they woke him up even at one o'clock in the afternoon. This caused a lot of tension in the house. The 'quid pro quo' strategy that was developed involved Sol's mother and sister accepting that it was Sol's decision how long he slept, and agreeing that they would not try to get him out of bed. In return, Sol agreed that he would not complain if he was woken up any time after eleven in the morning by the normal routine activity around the house.

Another example of a home-based strategy aimed to address negativity in discussions between family members involved using a 'table of positives'.

The table has the days of the week and the family members' names on it. Family members were to write against someone's name each day something they had done that they appreciated, which was polite or helpful. The following week, this was reviewed and a discussion was held in the session about the positives that were on the list and other positives that might have been included but had not been considered.

Another example involves the use of a borrowing register.

A family of four was involved in the family work—a mother and two sons, aged 12 and 13, and one daughter, aged 15. They reported that there were frequent shouting matches between the two boys over borrowing each other's possessions, in particular a DVD player and a computer. One of the boys suggested using a borrowing register. The register was to be placed on each of the boys' bedroom doors and they agreed to fill this out each time they borrowed something from each other. This proved to be very successful, and reduced the frequency and intensity of the arguments.

Sometimes home-based strategies discussed in sessions relate to practical issues such as accommodation.

A 15-year-old girl had been living in state care for two years after having continually run away from home following arguments with her mother. The young woman, Renee, had been placed in a number of hostels and spent a short period in foster care; however, each of the placements broke down largely because of Renee's behaviour, which included soiling and smearing her room.

She had been asked to leave her latest hostel placement, and her social worker indicated that she had no further options. She was given four weeks to find alternative accommodation. The social worker then worked through a series of Collaborative Family Work sessions with Renee and her mother and, after two sessions, a strategy was developed that involved Renee staying overnight at her mother's several times before she was to leave the hostel. Clear rules for the home stay were agreed upon within the Collaborative Family Work sessions. The Collaborative Family Work sessions subsequently led to a genuine reconciliation between mother and daughter, and Renee returned to live with her mother and was later discharged from state care.

Sometimes strategies involve a family member approaching others on behalf of another family member.

A problem identified by Yelena was that other family members did not care about her or take any interest in her. Yelena's mother suggested a strategy to show that she cared about her. The strategy involved the mother visiting Yelena at her work experience placement and talking to her supervisor about how she was going. Both Yelena and her mother agreed that this would help to show that her mother cared.

Strategies may relate to legal issues.

> A young man, Rafi, was released from a detention cen-
> tre and part of the condition of his parole was a curfew.
> Because he had offended with other young people, often
> late at night, he was required to be home each day before
> 8.00 p.m. He was not doing this, however, and this issue
> was identified by his mother in the family sessions. This
> was discussed in the session and it was agreed that, as a
> home strategy, Rafi and his mother would discuss this
> issue and work out a way in which Rafi could be home
> in time with the assistance of his mother, who could pick
> him up in her car at particular times. They were to report
> back on the decision they had reached in the next session.

In another example family members had a problem with
arguing and not listening to each other and they brainstormed strategies to address this. The workers then prepared
the following poster, which the family members displayed
on a wall at home (see Figure 7.4). This served as a reminder
to maintain a strategy of improved communication.

Worker strategies

Strategies may also be undertaken between sessions by
workers. As mentioned earlier, ideally family members will
suggest tasks for themselves and each other. In the same
way that workers might suggest strategies for the family,
family members might also suggest strategies to be carried
out by the worker. Workers might talk to school teachers,
get information about services, talk to a relative or arrange
financial assistance.

The following is an example of a worker strategy.

Figure 7.4: Strategies to improve communication

Problem: Communication
Issues
- Yelling
- Listening
- Arguing
- Over-reacting
- Bad behaviours
- Rudeness

How the family members have asked to talk to each other

- Use good manners
- Keep eye contact
- Be polite
- Use a good tone of voice
- Respect each other
- Listen to each other
- Be mindful of response

A 12-year-old boy, Daniel, wished to spend some weekends with his 20-year-old brother who lived independently. However, Daniel's mother was concerned that the brother had a number of undesirable friends who used drugs and had been in prison. The mother asked whether the worker could visit the brother to assess the situation and explain to him that he would have to accept responsibility for protecting Daniel from any negative influences from his associates. The worker was to report back at the next session.

Problem-related session strategies

Reference was made earlier to a number of session-based facilitative strategies—in other words, strategies that can be used to improve family communication but that are not directly linked to problems or goals. Some of these strategies can also be used in relation to specific problems, particularly if the issues of family communication or listening are identified as problems by family members. There are also many other strategies that can be used during sessions to address specific problems. Some of these strategies are outlined below.

Family members might be asked to *role-play* a situation in which arguments always seem to happen.

> A young man, Keppel, seemed to always argue with his father about cutting the grass around their home. The father would ask and ask, and Keppel would say later, later, not now. In exploring the problem with the worker, the father described how frustrated he was by having to continually yell at his son to cut the grass or do other things. Keppel, on the other hand, said that he wished his father would leave him alone and stop nagging him.
>
> The worker suggested role-playing the situation. Father and son then demonstrated through the role-play what typically happened. The worker then asked the father and Keppel to try doing it differently—to use an approach that might prevent the argument. The father asked politely and Keppel responded in a more positive manner. A home strategy was then set for Keppel and his father to use this positive manner the next time the grass needed to be cut.

Another approach to role-play involves role swapping, or family members playing each other's role. Continuing with the example above, the workers asked if Keppel and his father would reverse roles. They were then asked to discuss the situation regarding cutting the grass in a way that they felt was appropriate. This helped to give both father and son a better perspective in relation to each other's feelings about the issue.

Another way of approaching this strategy is for the workers to undertake a role-play in front of the family members. This is often done when the family work is conducted by two workers. In one instance, a problem of poor family communication had been identified. The family members felt that negative interactions often meant that individual family members did not get what they wanted. The two workers then undertook one role-play demonstrating a negative interaction and a second showing a positive interaction. This was followed by a discussion about the differences between the two conversations. They commented on the calmness, tone of voice, eye contact, openness, and willingness to listen and not judge which was evident in the positive role-play but not present in the negative one. The family members then commented that their interaction at home was more like the negative role-play. The family members said that they enjoyed the role-play, and a home-based strategy for dealing with disagreements was then developed modelled on the positive interaction demonstrated by the workers.

> In another complex family situation, a teenage girl, 15-year-old Pari, had an intellectual disability and a diagnosed mental illness, as well as problems with illegal drug use, acting out sexual behaviour, regularly staying out all night and truancy. She was under the care of the

state, but continued to live intermittently with her family. Two workers worked with Pari and her mother and sister. One session strategy involved Pari's goal to live independently away from home, and a discussion was held between all family members present regarding possible options, including living with her father or in a placement through child protection. When this discussion had been exhausted, Pari decided to change her goal from living away from home to living at home, but in a more enjoyable way. A further session strategy was then undertaken with all family members about how this could be achieved, and this led to a further session-based strategy that involved the development of house rules.

In this particular family, a session-based strategy of using a message stick was also introduced in response to an identified problem of family members talking over each other. Family members and the workers could only speak in session if they held the message stick. This helped them to develop the habit of not talking when others were speaking, and allowing others to have a turn to speak.

Sometimes strategies relate to issues that have caused hurt within families.

An issue was raised in one family in relation to Con, a young man who had committed a series of criminal offences. He was referred to family work by a court. When undertaking the problem identification, three other family members—mother, father and sister—each identified the issue of Con's offending as a problem for them. They said it had torn their family apart over many years, and until it stopped the family would have little peace. Con listened to this and said that he had not realised how much his family members were concerned. He suggested a home task that involved asking the family members to tell him about what his offending had meant to them and how differently they felt now that he had stopped (Con had not been arrested for more than six months). In the following session, Con said he was amazed at how much pain the family members had experienced and how much better they felt today because he had stopped offending.

Another example of a problem-based session strategy related to the inability of family members to follow rules when they were at home. The family members brainstormed family rules, and the workers wrote these down and then had them typed up in a display that the family members could take home with them. The family rules are shown in Figure 7.5.

Figure 7.5: Family rules

- Respect each other's property.
- Dry ourselves in the bathroom.
- No backchatting.
- No swearing.
- Look after our house.
- Have quiet time in the late afternoon.
- Listen to each other.
- Have quiet time in the morning until everyone is awake.

What if strategies are not carried out?

If a strategy is not carried out, as discussed earlier, this should not be seen as the fault of any family member; rather, it is a problem with the strategy. A discussion can be held regarding why it was not carried out. Workers and family members can address the following questions: Did all family members understand what was to be done? Was the task clearly defined? Was it too hard? Did family members really agree to it? Did it overload one or two family members? Did other factors intervene that prevented the task from being carried out? Following this discussion, the task can either be discarded and new tasks developed or the task can be redefined so that it can be attempted again.

Sometimes strategies are carried out but they do not solve the problem. In these instances, the same process can be used to examine why the problem was not solved. It should be noted, however, that sometimes even when tasks do not solve the immediate presenting problem, the process of carrying them out may be beneficial. In one example, even though the listening strategy had not solved the presenting problems of the number of arguments between the family members, each of the family members felt that they had more awareness of their own feelings and increased empathy for the person they were arguing with. In other words, while nothing had changed, the family members felt better and they understood more about what was going on. This is a finding consistent with the theory behind cognitive behavioural interventions, discussed in Chapter 2. The degree of impact that problems have on people is related to how the problems are perceived as well as the nature of the problem.

It is also clear that some family problems are simply able

to be solved. Past sexual abuse, violence, poverty, lack of education and discrimination may not be solved by developing strategies in a family work session. Often, however, the ways in which people feel about these things can change. This is not to say that Collaborative Family Work does not generally lead to improved outcomes for families—just that sometimes what is learnt from the process may be just as valuable as the specific outcome.

Identifying obstacles to strategies

In order to reduce the likelihood of strategies not being carried out, workers should explore potential obstacles. Sometimes there are specific practical obstacles to the implementation of strategies.

> Seb, a 15-year-old boy, and his mother, Ursula, decided they would like to work on communication issues. Their goal was to improve their rating on the problem rating scale for communication from 2 to 4. Seb and Ursula agreed that if the rating was 4 they would talk to each other in a civil manner and spend some time together on a regular basis, and argue once a week rather than the current ten or 20 times a week.
>
> One of the agreed tasks was for them to visit the zoo together. The worker then explored potential obstacles: Was there a time when Ursula could get away from work for at least two hours to go to the zoo? Which day suited them both, given that Seb also had some regular activities with his case manager and an employment program? Was the zoo expensive and did they have the money to pay? Were other members of the family—in particular, Seb's younger brother—to come along as

well, and would this still provide the opportunity for Seb and his mother to talk to each other? Was the visit dependent on the weather? Was there a substitute activity they could do if it rained?

Exploration of potential obstacles in this way can help to increase the likelihood that the tasks will be successful.

Integration with other services

Collaborative Family Work is designed for work with people involved in the human services, whether in child protection, family welfare, mental health, drug treatment, juvenile justice, adult corrections, school welfare or medical support services. In many cases, those involved in Collaborative Family Work will also be involved with other agencies.

> A young offender, Kieran, was involved with a mental health service, where he was seeing a psychiatrist, a mental health social worker and a volunteer mentor. He was also involved in an employment transition program, which was helping him to prepare for and obtain work. He was also involved with a voluntary agency that was providing support to his family and included a family social worker and personal helper for his disabled sister. In addition to this, he was on probation and was required to see his probation officer on a weekly basis.

In some cases, there will be a designated case manager who will take responsibility for planning and integrating services. In some systems, this is a statutory worker such as a probation officer, child protection worker or mental health worker. Often, however, as previously discussed, clients in the human services systems are confused about the role of the various services and the services are disconnected from each other. It is not within the scope of this book to discuss the issues surrounding case management in any detail. Suffice to say that when working with families, strategies will have more chance of success if the worker understands what else is being done with the family by other human service workers. In the example of Seb and Ursula, it could be that Seb's case manager is working to help him to separate from his mother and increase his levels of independence. In this case, the strategy of spending time at the zoo might be inappropriate. Gaining a general picture of the agencies involved with the family will help to ensure that the strategies that are put in place complement work done by other agencies. Information about other agencies can be gathered in discussions about potential obstacles as well as during the problem-exploration stage.

Strategies need to be culturally appropriate

Collaborative Family Work has been developed in work with families from many different cultures, including Aboriginal families in rural and remote regions of Australia. It has been used in Australia with African, Indian, Southeast Asian, European, Chinese and South American families. It has been used in the United Kingdom with families from a range of different cultures. Work has also been done using similar models with Afro-American families in the United States (Reid 1985) and in Tehran (Ahmadi et al. 2010). Collaborative Family Work is suited to work with different cultures because it involves teaching families to solve their own problems. Family members identify the problems, family members decide what they wish to achieve and family members set the strategies. Family members themselves can therefore determine what is culturally appropriate and what is not.

On the other hand, as discussed earlier, there are certain assumptions on which Collaborative Family Work is based. It is assumed that family members can and will allow each other to speak free of intimidation or threats of violence. It is assumed that one or two family members will not dominate the sessions to the extent that others cannot get a word in. It is assumed that a reasonably equitable exchange of views is possible. In the development of strategies, these principles continue to apply.

Workers should encourage strategies that break down inequitable family structures. For example, the parents of an 18-year-old woman were concerned about their daughter wanting to go out alone without a chaperone. The worker saw the parents' views as a reflection of a particular culture and encouraged problem definition, goals and strategies that reflected a more 'Western' approach to this issue. The worker suggested a strategy of inviting a young man to come to dinner with the family. In another example, a man restricted the ability of his wife to have friends or go to social occasions, and she agreed to this because it was part of her cultural expectations. The worker, however, encouraged strategies that involved the woman having more social interaction.

Case study: Exploring problems and developing strategies

Worker: Now I think we're doing very well with this
            process. I think it's terrific that you've been

	here now for three sessions. Rebekah, how are you finding it so far?
Rebekah:	It's okay.
Worker:	You'll be happier if we can work out some of these problems, won't you?
Rebekah:	Mmm hmm.
Ilana:	We had a bit of a yelling match about the dad thing during the week.
Worker:	Did you?
Ilana:	Yeah.
Worker:	Well, that's what we want to talk about today.
Ilana:	So we're going to spend an hour talking about Dad?
Worker:	Well, about the problems with listening and the problems with seeing your dad, Rebekah.
Ilana:	It'll probably take me an hour to talk about how crap he is . . .
Worker:	Okay (to Rebekah), what you're saying is you'd like to see your dad three or four times a week.
Rebekah:	Mmm hmm (nodding).
Worker:	That's a point of disagreement with you, but that's Rebekah's goal.
Ilana:	Yeah, well, we sort of argued about it, so . . .
Worker:	You have, okay, and your goal, of course, is for Rebekah to listen to you and to talk to you and be involved in the things around the house.
Ilana:	Yeah, well, I think that if she listened to me, then maybe she'd understand a bit more about why I think she shouldn't see her dad.
Worker:	But she has been listening to you, hasn't she, in these sessions?
Ilana:	I don't know if she's been listening or not. I suppose she has, because I must admit she set the table once during the week.

Worker:	Good! That's great. What happened there, Rebekah?
Rebekah:	I'm not sure.
Worker:	Was your mum nice to you?
Rebekah:	Yes.
Worker:	So things might be improving a bit?
Ilana:	Well, I don't know. What do you think?
Rebekah:	(Shrugs)
Worker:	Well let's start. Can we start talking about your father? And then we'll come on to the listening. So we're dealing with two problems here. But it's very important to you, seeing your father, isn't it, Rebekah?
Rebekah:	(Nods).
Worker:	Can you talk a bit about the past and what's happened with your dad, and the problems . . .
Ilana:	And don't lie.
Worker:	You went to see him and he wasn't there and things like that. How long ago did he leave?
Rebekah:	I'm not sure.
Ilana:	He hasn't been around for ages.
Worker:	And so when was the first time you saw him, Rebekah?
Rebekah:	(Shrugs).
Ilana:	It was about when you were 8. It's only been the last three years that he's started to see you. He didn't give a crap for the first few years.
Worker:	Okay, so you've been going to see him for a few years now?
Rebekah:	Mmm (Nods).
Worker:	And can you tell me a bit about him? About your dad?
Rebekah:	(Hesitates).
Ilana:	Go on.

Rebekah:	Well . . .
Worker:	Do you like him a lot?
Rebekah:	Yes.
Worker:	What do you do with him when you go there?
Ilana:	Sit and play on the telly, play Nintendo. I bet. I bet.
Rebekah:	No, we go on walks, we go to the park. Sometimes we go to the movies.
Worker:	Do you? He takes you to the movies?
Rebekah:	Mmmm.
Worker:	And he's got a new partner? A girlfriend?
Rebekah:	No, not yet.
Worker:	He hasn't?
Ilana:	He's probably had about five . . . ten . . . in the last three years.
Worker:	Okay. Alright. So he's living on his own?
Rebekah:	Yes.
Worker:	So was there a problem with you going there and him not being there?
Rebekah:	No.
Ilana:	There was. There was. You used to come home crying because he wasn't there.
Worker:	So, would you drop Rebekah off and he wouldn't be there?
Ilana:	Well, he hadn't been around for ages and then all of a sudden he wanted to start seeing her, so I thought, well okay. There's no court orders, no nothing, because he's never even bothered to go to court. So I thought okay, I'll be nice, she was 8, she really wanted to see him. So the first time I took her there and dropped her off, and that was fine. And then, every time I dropped her off she'd come home and there'd be a bit more attitude. So

	I thought, well no, I'm not going to take you, and I kept telling him if he wants to see her he should go to court and he's never bothered. So why should I make an effort? So now obviously she's been sneaking off and seeing him herself.
Worker:	(To Rebekah) But you're saying that it's good—when you go, he's there?
Rebekah:	Mmmm.
Worker:	Does he know you're coming? Do you tell him when you're going to come?
Rebekah:	No.
Worker:	You just turn up? Is there a particular time when you know he's going to be home?
Rebekah:	Yeah.
Worker:	So you go to the park? What other . . .
Rebekah:	We go to the movies and we go shopping because he gives me stuff so . . .
Worker:	He gives you stuff. And it sounds like you're quite good friends with him. You like him a lot?
Rebekah:	Yeah.
Worker:	Do you argue with him?
Rebekah:	No, never.
Worker:	You don't?
Ilana:	So how long have you been going to see him?
Rebekah:	None of your business.
Worker:	Well, we were going to be honest, weren't we, Rebekah?
Rebekah:	Well, she can't find out everything about me.
Worker:	Okay, well that's up to you.
Ilana:	I just want to know when you've been going. Has it been during school or after school?
Rebekah:	After school.

Worker:	So you know a time when he's going to be home. Is he working, your dad?
Rebekah:	Ummm, sometimes, but most of the time he isn't.
Worker:	Okay.
Ilana:	Yeah, probably he just works every now and then. I can't even imagine him staying at work.
Worker:	And does he treat you well? He's kind to you?
Rebekah:	Mmmhmm (nods).
Worker:	Okay, so what can we do about this? I mean, what's your view about this, Ilana?
Ilana:	Well, I don't know why he wants to see her. He's never wanted to since she was 2, when he left. All of a sudden he wants to see her. I reckon it's because he's got no job anymore and he just wants to get something out of her.
Worker:	What's your worry about . . . ?
Ilana:	I don't know. When she comes back, her attitude is worse. I don't know why.
Worker:	Now, is that the case, or don't you know when she's been?
Ilana:	I don't know, maybe that's why her attitude has changed. Maybe in the last few years she's been sneaking out. Maybe that's why she's been as she is. Because it wasn't happening before. She was a lovely person before. And now she's saying that for the last two years she's been seeing him, and that's when her behaviour changed. Maybe it's because she's sneaking off and seeing him.
Worker:	Well I think it's a natural thing for an 11-year-old girl to want to see her father, isn't it?
Ilana:	I suppose so.
Worker:	So what do you think? Let's look at how we can deal with this. Obviously she's very upset

Ilana:	and getting angry with you. Is there some compromise?
	Well, shouldn't the courts sort that out? Why doesn't he go to court and sort it out?
Worker:	Well that's one option. Would it help if I spoke to your father? Would you like me to go and talk to him?
Ilana:	You won't get him to see you!
Worker:	Do you think he'd talk to me, Rebekah?
Rebekah:	Yes.
Ilana:	You think he would talk to a stranger? Go ahead, try.
Worker:	Well, I could certainly talk to him and I could give you some information about . . .
Ilana:	But you won't tell him about what we've been talking about?
Worker:	No, no . . . I can introduce myself as someone from the Family Support Services. How would you feel about that, Rebekah?
Ilana:	But then he'll think that I'm a hopeless mum and then he will go to court and use the fact that we've had to come and see you against me in court.
Worker:	Okay, this is a suggestion, that's all. I would just talk to him about . . .
Ilana:	Well, I want you to tell me, how I can let an 11-year-old girl go and see her dad when maybe he won't be there?
Worker:	Well I think it's fair enough for you to have some information about whether or not he's there. Don't you think that's fair, Rebekah? I mean, your mum is worried about you going off and not knowing where you are. She may be much more happy about you going to see your dad if she knows that your dad's actually

	going to be there. So are you, Ilana, in a position to talk to Rebekah's father?
Ilana:	Ummm, well, I don't really want to see him.
Worker:	When's the last time you spoke to him?
Ilana:	Oh, ages ago. Because he's never rung up and asked to see her. In the last year or so he's never asked. But now I know why, obviously, because she's been sneaking out and seeing him.
Worker:	And she likes to see him.
Ilana:	I mean, tell me, don't you think a responsible dad should have rung the mum and said: 'Do you know your daughter's coming to see me?'
Worker:	Yes, I think that's fair enough. It's probably got something to do with your relationship with each other, but . . . we have the situation now where Rebekah wants very much to see her dad. She's getting very angry with you. Is there some compromise?
Ilana:	Well if she listens to me about what I'm worried about when she goes and sees him. And if she listens to me when she comes back from seeing him, if her attitude's okay, well then, maybe . . . , maybe . . .
Worker:	How do you feel about that, Rebekah?
Rebekah:	Well, it's just a maybe and usually her maybes are nos.
Worker:	So what she's saying is that she could arrange for you to see your dad if when you come back you're okay and listen to your mum—if you don't come back in a sort of angry state. Well, maybe we could try something like this?
Rebekah:	(Shrugs) Don't ask me, ask her.
Worker:	Well, your mum's saying she's concerned

	about you going off to your dad's and then coming back angry with her. Does this happen?
Ilana:	I don't reckon you're having such a good time, or else you'd be okay when you came back.
Rebekah:	I am fine.
Worker:	So do you feel that you get angry with your mum after seeing your dad?
Rebekah:	Yes, because after my dad's been so nice to me, then Mum is mean to me.
Ilana:	All I do is ask you where you've been and you say, whatever, and go away. That's all I do.
Worker:	Well, what's your suggestion? Do you two have a suggestion as to how we can sort this out because at the moment it's not working, is it? Rebekah's seeing her dad anyway, it's causing a lot of arguments, Rebekah's getting very angry. What are we going to do?
Ilana:	Well, maybe . . . I can't believe I'm saying this, but . . . maybe if I ring him and say: 'Okay, can she come over on the weekend for a couple of hours?' And that's it. And I'll drop her off. And make sure that he's there, and I'll pick her up. But I don't want to see him. I'll make sure she goes in the door and that's it.
Worker:	And how do you feel about that, Rebekah?
Rebekah:	Yeah, I'm fine with that.
Ilana:	And she's got to promise me that when I pick her up she won't have an attitude, and she'll just listen to me, and answer things that I ask.
Worker:	So we're going to try that this weekend? On Saturday?
Rebekah:	(Nods).
Ilana:	Yes, alright . . . yes.

Worker:	So, Ilana, you're going to contact him. If this doesn't work, and you want me to be involved, we can talk about it?
Ilana:	Well I don't want you talking to him because then he'll think that we have got real problems. He'll say: 'Oh, you had to go and see the welfare and . . . ' So, look, I'll give it a go. But if he's rude to me on the phone, I can't guarantee that I'll get through it.
Worker:	So, Ilana is going to contact your father and try and arrange for you to visit and she'll drop you there and pick you up. And we'll try this on a trial for this Saturday. And we'll see how it goes.
Ilana:	And promise me that you won't bitch and be a cow once you come back from him.
Rebekah:	Okay! Fine.
Worker:	And then when I come back next week, we'll look at how it's gone and we'll look at a further plan for seeing him more regularly. The other issue is this listening and arguing and jobs around the house. Can we talk about that for a while?
Ilana:	She said if she sees her dad then she will start listening.
Rebekah:	Yeah.
Worker:	Okay, but we need to be a bit more specific about what the problem is and what you're expecting and what you mean by not listening, what the chores are that have to be done. So you both agree on what it is that you want to do. So you've got one thing to do and maybe Rebekah might have one thing to do.
Ilana:	So, you're saying that if I let her see her dad,

	then maybe she could set the table. All I want her to do is set the table for the whole week without arguing with me.
Worker:	Well, what I'm saying is, we've sorted out one thing to happen in relation to Dad. Let's talk a bit about the other problem, the listening, and see if we can get a strategy. That might be one, if Rebekah agreed to that.
Ilana:	OK, well ask her—what will she do? What will you do (to Rebekah)?
Rebekah:	I'm not sure.
Ilana:	Well surely you can think of something you can do.
Rebekah:	Well, I'll do the chores you want me to do.
Ilana:	So you're saying that you'll make your bed, keep your room tidy and set the table all week.
Worker:	I'm just wondering whether we might try something. Let's say you want Rebekah to help you with the dinner?
Ilana:	That'd be great. That'd be great if she helped me with dinner.
Worker:	So what usually happens when you ask Rebekah something?
Ilana:	Well, if I asked her to do anything around the house, she'd just go 'Whatever!' and walk away and not do it. And I'd yell at her and say 'Come back here, I need you to do this.' And she'd just get angry at me.
Worker:	So do you think we could try a little practice exercise? Would you be willing just to try to answer it in a different way? Doing it in a way that your mum would like you to?
Rebekah:	Okay.
Worker:	So let's try it. Ilana, you're going to just

imagine you're at home and you've come
home from work and you're busy and
frazzled, and you're saying to Rebekah, can
you help me with . . . what . . . peeling the
potatoes or something like that?

Ilana: Yes, okay.

Worker: Okay, so let's try it. And Rebekah, can you
just try, don't just be your usual self but
try it in a way that might make your mum
happier, so that you wouldn't have an
argument. Our aim is to stop the argument
happening here.

Rebekah: Yes.

Worker: Will you try that, Ilana?

Ilana: You want us to do it now?

Worker: Yes, if that's okay.

Ilana: Rebekah, come and help me with dinner. I've
just got home from work and I'm tired. Could
you please go and do the potatoes?

Rebekah: Okay.

Ilana: You're going to say okay?

Rebekah: Yeah.

Ilana: You'll just go and do them?

Rebekah: Yeah.

Worker: OK, so Rebekah, what your mum just said
then, was that okay or would you like her to
have said that differently?

Rebekah: (Shrugs).

Worker: Could you say that again, Ilana, in a way that
is sort of more . . . well, I think that the way
you said it was fair enough, but maybe try in
a way that is a bit more friendly, and a bit less
likely to make Rebekah react?

Ilana: Alright. You want me to do it now? Rebekah,
could you please peel the potatoes for me?

	I've got to get your dinner ready and I'm really tired and it would be great if you could peel the potatoes for me.
Rebekah:	Yes, sure.
Worker:	Is that how she usually says it, Rebekah, or does she say it in a different way?
Rebekah:	No, she says it in a yelling way, like: 'Rebekah, go do the potatoes. I need you to go cook dinner for me.' And then I say no.
Worker:	So if she were to say it the way she did just then, it would be better, would it?
Rebekah:	Yeah.
Worker:	And would you then help with the dinner?
Rebekah:	Yeah . . . probably.
Worker:	Well, I wonder if we can try that this week? Your mum's agreed to talk to your dad and set up to go over there on Saturday. And you are going to do that?
Ilana:	Yes.
Worker:	After you speak to Dad, Ilana, if there's any problem, can you give me a ring and let me know?
Ilana:	So if I ring up on Wednesday and he's like he normally is—an arrogant little . . .
Worker:	If you find a problem and you can't sort it out, if you could ring me and let me know. And the listening issue?
Ilana:	I'm happy to ask her in a nice, happy, polite way. But I wouldn't guarantee that she'd still do it. But I'm happy to do that, just to prove my point, that she won't do it, that even if I'm nice to her, she won't do it.
Worker:	Okay. So, Rebekah, if she asks you in a nice, polite, reasonable way, then you'll just say, 'Okay Mum' like you just did then?

Rebekah:	Yep.
Worker:	So we'll try that. I mean, it may not work, and if it doesn't work then we'll review it and look at why it didn't work.
Rebekah:	Well, I mean, I'm only going to say 'Yes, okay' if my dad says I can come over. I mean, that's the only reason why I'm going to do it.
Ilana:	But I can't make him say yes. I'll ask him and I'll be as polite as possible, and hopefully he'll say yes, if he wants to see you.
Worker:	Well, we're going to see.
Ilana:	Well, maybe she should be listening when I make the phone call?
Worker:	Yes . . .
Rebekah:	Yeah (Nods).
Ilana:	So that she knows that it's not me if he says no.
Worker:	So your mum's going to ring your dad when you are there. And she's also agreed to try to talk to you in a nicer way about the jobs around the house. And then you've agreed that if she's nice to you, to do the things that she's asked and listen to her. So if it all works out, then everything will be terrific. If it doesn't work out, then we'll have to look at why it didn't work out.
Ilana:	Sounds okay.
Worker:	I think we're getting somewhere really, because the way you're talking to each other now, it's a lot better than happens at home, isn't it?
Ilana and Rebekah: Yes.	

Strategies for Ilana and Rebekah for this week
- Ilana to ring Rebekah's father and speak

> to him politely about Rebekah visiting him.
> If he is agreeable, drive Rebekah to her
> father's and pick her up two hours later.
> * Rebekah to be present when Ilana rings.
> * Ilana to ask Rebekah in a friendly and
>   pleasant way to do her jobs around the
>   house.
> * Rebekah to listen to her mother and set
>   the table when she asks.

This transcript begins with a brief discussion about how things have been going and a summary of what has been agreed on so far. It has been decided to work on two issues—one for Rebekah (seeing her father) and one for Ilana (regarding Rebekah listening and doing things around the house). Two issues were chosen to work on rather than one because this seemed to the worker to be more equitable as Rebekah and Ilana had different priorities. The worker then begins to explore the issue related to Rebekah seeing her father and then encourages Ilana and Rebekah to come up with a strategy to address the problem. Once the strategy of mother contacting father has been raised, potential obstacles are explored. The worker also suggests contacting them again if anything goes wrong.

A similar approach is then taken to the mother's problem of listening and Rebekah's reluctance to help with chores around the house. A session-based problem strategy is used to help Rebekah and Ilana develop a different way of interacting when Ilana asks Rebekah to help with household chores.

The worker has some concerns that Rebekah's father might provide an unsuitable environment for her, and this was one reason for offering to contact him. Ilana did not like this idea; however, her involvement may provide some protection for Rebekah if the care provided by the father is inappropriate.

The transcript of the Rebekah/Ilana interview in this and earlier chapters is, of course, provided as an illustration of a Collaborative Family Work intervention and is not complete. It includes the equivalent of only ten minutes of a family work session that might have taken about 45 minutes. There is no exploration of Ilana's problem of Rebekah not listening to her, for example. Nevertheless, it aims to provide an idea of how the sessions might work.

Chapter summary

This chapter outlined problem exploration and the development of strategies. The strategies or tasks, as they are sometimes referred to, were divided into session-based facilitative strategies, home-based facilitative strategies, problem-related session strategies and problem-related home strategies. This was followed by a discussion about addressing obstacles to the implementation of strategies, the need for strategies to fit with other services and the need for strategies to be culturally appropriate. The next stage in the Rebekah and Ilana case study was also included.

8

Reviewing and concluding the family work sessions

This chapter focuses on the need for ongoing review in each session, the way the final session can be used to maintain the gains that have been made and how the family work can be evaluated. It also provides a real-life case study of a Collaborative Family Work intervention.

Ongoing review

As each step in the model is carried out, progress in relation to that step should be reviewed on a routine basis. For example, at the start of each session it is common to review progress in relation to any tasks that have been undertaken between sessions. It is also common to review what occurred in earlier sessions. Ground rules, for example, are usually typed up by the worker between sessions and then displayed in subsequent sessions. It is usually appropriate to go over the ground rules at the beginning of the early sessions and ensure that everyone still agrees with them. Similarly, reviews of problem lists or goals or strategies may be undertaken at the beginning of each session. These reviews can be integrated with the process of using the rating scales to rate general family functioning and progress in relation to specific problems. The process of ongoing review is important to help family members and workers to understand which stage they are at in the model, and to understand that changes may be made to ground rules, problem lists, goals or strategies as family members progress through the family work process.

It has been pointed out throughout this book that Collaborative Family Work is a flexible model. The model has clear steps, and these steps need to be reviewed as workers and family members progress through the model. It has been emphasised that at any given time the worker and the family members should be able to identify the stage they are at in the model. However, it is also important that workers and family members move around within the model as appropriate. For example, it may be that a session is focused on a particular issue and another issue arises in discussion. To take an actual case example, a family was developing strategies to develop listening skills when the mother mentioned for the first time that the family was soon to face eviction from its accommodation. The worker and the family members then returned to the problem survey, discussed where accommodation fitted in terms of priority in comparison to other issues on the problem lists, and decided that this issue was more pressing than any other. They then considered goals in relation to accommodation, explored the issue and began to develop strategies.

The final session

The final session provides an opportunity for the worker and family members to review progress and to set in place plans to maintain the gains that the family has made. For example, a family may have started with family functioning at 2 on the five-point scale and by the last session it might be 4. The workers can then ask the family members to identify what is different now compared with when they started the family work. For example, family members may say that they now listen to each other more. The worker can then briefly explore with the family how this has happened and how the family members can make sure they do not return to the previous pattern of not listening to each other. A discussion can be held about what strategies can be used in the future, without the benefit of the family work sessions, to encourage family members to continue listening to each other. This might involve continuing some strategies they have used previously or identifying new strategies. The aim in the final session is to leave the family members with a set of strategies to help them to maintain the gains that they have made.

Family members can also be asked what they will do if the problems that led them into family work resurface. If, for example, the family functioning deteriorates, and family members begin to feel that they are not being listened to, what can be done? Are there strategies that individual family members might use to address the issue? Can they return for further family work sessions? The circumstances under which further family work might be offered should be discussed.

Evaluation

The final step in the Collaborative Family Work model involves the worker evaluating the intervention in discussion with the family members. The purpose of the evaluation is twofold. First, it provides an opportunity for family members to say what they think about the model and about the service that has been offered to them. This process acknowledges family members' expertise in knowing what helps them. The evaluation can also help the worker to understand whether the family work has been successful, from the perspective of each of the family members. It can also help the worker to understand which aspects of the work family members feel have been most effective and which aspects least effective. The evaluation can in turn help the worker to continually improve their skills and to improve the family work offered in subsequent interventions—consistent with the concept of reflective practice referred to in Chapter 2 (Knott & Scagg 2010). It can also provide an opportunity for organisations to gather data and thereby monitor not only the work of individual workers but also that of the organisation.

I have chosen to finish the book with an actual case study taken in part from an earlier publication (Trotter, Cox & Crawford 2002). The family work was undertaken in a juvenile justice setting by workers who had received 24 hours of training in Collaborative Family Work. They also had the benefit of ongoing supervision while they worked with the family. While this is an actual case study, like the other case studies in this book, important details have been changed to ensure that those involved cannot be recognised.

Case study: Arun

Arun lived with his father, Darwin. He was 16 years old and during the past twelve months had appeared in court on several occasions for multiple car thefts and property offences. Immediately prior to being referred for family work, Arun had appeared in court following a number of further thefts of motor vehicles. The court requested a pre-sentence report from the local Juvenile Justice Centre.

The juvenile justice worker who was preparing the pre-sentence report then referred the family for family work. She believed that there were problems within the family relationships that might have led to Arun's offending. She felt that Arun might be harbouring anger towards his mother. She also felt that a pattern had emerged within the family whereby Arun would offend and then receive a lot of negative attention from his father. The offending would then cease, tension between them would again build, and eventually Arun would reoffend. Darwin would then again concentrate his efforts upon his son.

Arun's mother had left the family home about a year before, and now lived within walking distance of the home. The mother was not involved in the family work and the juvenile justice worker who referred the family suggested that the mother was an alcoholic. Arun's younger sister, Penny, lived with her mother, although she often returned to the father's house when her mother's drinking became excessive.

Arun's offending began soon after his mother left home. The juvenile justice worker felt that the offending might also be related to this or to Arun's use of drugs. However, the drug issue was never clarified and did not arise as a problem during the family work sessions. Darwin said that he was very keen to help Arun, but he felt he had tried everything and had reached the point of exasperation. He was considering asking Arun to leave home.

Seven sessions were held with Arun and Darwin over a period of eight weeks. The family work is presented here as it happened. No attempt has been made to embellish it or present it as it should have happened. Each of the sessions was conducted in the family home in the early evening. During the first session, Penny arrived halfway through. She sat in on the remainder of that session without participating and chose not to be involved in future sessions. The family work subsequently only involved two family members.

In the initial session, the workers explained that they would be using the Collaborative Family Work model to help the family with their problems. Each of the steps of the model was explained. To help the family understand the model, the workers placed a large poster of the steps of the model on a wall in the family home so that the family and the workers could follow their progress through the various steps. This poster was displayed in all sessions.

Issues around confidentiality were discussed, and the role of the two workers was explained. Ground rules that would apply to all sessions were discussed with Arun and Darwin and then written down by the workers. These included having equal time to speak during sessions, not answering for each other, listening without interrupting, not blaming each other and committing to attend each session. These ground rules were set in the initial session and remained unchanged throughout the remaining sessions.

During the first session, the workers asked Arun and

Darwin to talk about the issues or problems that most concerned them. Arun talked about why he stole cars. He said he felt an 'urge' to offend that he could not control. He said he was not doing well at school and that he was bored in his spare time. He said he felt his father did not trust him.

Darwin expressed frustration at the offending. He was most concerned about not being able to trust Arun. He saw himself as the 'policeman'. He was also concerned that Arun would sneak out or take money if it was left around.

Arun and Darwin were asked during the initial session to rate the level of family functioning on a five-point scale from very poor (1) to very good (5). They both provided a rating of 3—in other words, the family functioning was: 'Satisfactory—family members communicate on some issues and there is some satisfaction in family life although things could be a lot better'. Both workers felt that Arun and Darwin were minimising the extent of their problems.

During the initial session, one worker would lead the session and the second worker would take notes. These notes were written in large letters on a piece of paper by the worker after checking with Arun and Darwin that they were an accurate reflection of what was being said. The notes in the first session listed each of the problems underneath Arun's or Darwin's name. Darwin then placed the notes on the wall in the living room where the sessions took place. The notes were added to each week, and were not taken down for the duration of the sessions. They remained in place between sessions.

During the second session, an attempt was made to

reach agreement on which problems it would be best to address first. Arun and Darwin identified the following problems as issues they would like to work on:

- Arun's urge to offend
- Darwin's inability to trust Arun
- Arun's concern that his father did not listen to him or understand him and continually lectured him
- The way Arun and Darwin spent their spare time
- Arun's school

The workers had concerns about the lack of communication between Arun and his father, but did not raise this specifically. The workers decided to wait and see whether this issue would emerge later.

Arun's urge to offend by stealing motor vehicles was identified as the most pressing problem for both Arun and Darwin. The discussions relating to this particular problem only are reported below. At the end of the second session, Arun and Darwin were asked to rate the seriousness of the problem relating to offending. Darwin rated it as a serious problem, giving it a rating of 2.5 on the five-point scale. Despite having raised the issue as a problem, Arun rated it at 5—in other words, 'There is no real problem'. Both workers felt that Arun was minimising the issue and that his rating on this scale reflected his ambivalence about being involved in the family work process.

The workers then moved into the problem-exploration stage and encouraged Arun to more fully explore the 'urge to offend'. Arun felt that he was more likely to offend when he was bored or when he was with mates who stole cars. He said that he enjoyed the 'rush' he experienced when he was driving. However, he stated that he did not speed because that was 'stupid and you could kill someone'. The workers became aware of some inconsistencies in Arun's statements, and believed that Arun was concerned about admitting that he sped in front of his father. The workers had concerns about how truthful Arun was being generally. He appeared keen to please his father.

At one stage, Arun stated that because he was dealing with this particular aspect of the problem (his urge to offend) with his juvenile justice worker, he would rather deal with other things in the family sessions. Nonetheless, he agreed after some further discussion to continue to explore this issue.

During further exploration in the third session, two underlying reasons for Arun's offending emerged. The first was anger or annoyance and the other was poor communication about 'little' things and the frustration he felt because of this. Arun said that he tended to be quick to react when he was angry, hitting out physically rather than talking about how he felt. He talked about instances when he hit someone following a short, heated verbal exchange. This problem of Arun's anger was then added to the list of problems that Arun had earlier identified. Arun's anger was seen as a problem by both Arun and his father, and it was added to the father's list along with the issues of trust and Arun's urge to steal. Discussion then focused on Arun's anger rather than his urge to offend. It was felt by the workers and by Arun and Darwin that Arun's anger and his urge to offend were closely related, and Arun indicated that he would prefer to work on the anger issue rather than the urge to offend.

At this stage, there was some attempt by the workers to broach the subject of the relationship between Arun and his mother (and Darwin and his wife), but they were not willing to explore it. Again consistent with the model, the workers did not press the point.

Developing tasks/strategies

In Session 4, the counsellors attempted to develop with Arun and Darwin a number of strategies to deal with the problem of Arun's anger. Arun suggested a physical outlet. Maybe go-karting or other fast, risky activities could achieve the 'rush' that he sought when he offended. However, as these were expensive and not immediately available, it was suggested by the workers that something like a punching bag or gym work might be more effective. Darwin was resistant to the punching bag but more supportive of Arun going to a gym. This was discussed and set as a task (although it was not acted upon during the counselling period).

A verbal outlet for anger was also explored. Darwin talked about his own way of dealing with people when he was angry. He suggested that he experienced feelings in a similar way to Arun but had learnt over his lifetime that he could not just hit out at people. He spoke of strategies such as calling them names when they were out of earshot or using a physical outlet such as walking. He said he still blew up at people, but did it much less often now. While no specific strategy emerged from this discussion, both Arun and Darwin were involved in it and it seemed to help their understanding of each other.

Discussion followed about the need for Arun to practise expressing his feelings. Arun suggested that he would like his father to listen to him without immediately lecturing him, and generally show more appreciation of him. He felt this would make him less angry. A task suggested by the workers was agreed to. Arun would carry out a particular activity that he felt his father would appreciate (such as mowing the lawn). He would then explain to his father that he had done it to help him. Darwin agreed that when this occurred he would express his appreciation and resist the temptation to tell Arun how it could have been done better.

In the next session, Arun and Darwin reported that this task had partly worked. Arun did some work in the garden and planted some flowers, but he had been unable to clearly verbalise to his father that he had done this for him. The situation was discussed and the task was modified for the next week.

Arun was to do something—perhaps wash the car—and say to Darwin: 'I did that for you'. Darwin agreed to accept this action as a show of appreciation and in turn he was to say something appreciative to Arun about it. He also agreed to show appreciation of Arun in some other way during the week.

During the next session, both Arun and his father reported that the tasks were carried out and that they were both very happy with how they went. Arun did in fact wash the car, his father did show appreciation and Arun said that this made him feel happier and less angry.

While these tasks may seem relatively small steps in terms of dealing with Arun's and Darwin's issues, the workers felt that a lot of Arun's problems stemmed from his relationship with his father and from his father's dismissive attitude. The workers felt that the increased communication between Arun and Darwin, and Darwin's willingness to express his appreciation to his son, were big steps towards helping Arun control his anger and his offending.

Final evaluation

In the final session, Arun and Darwin were asked again to rate the level of functioning within the family. Both Arun and Darwin rated this at 4. In other words, 'It is very satisfactory and basically things are okay within the family'—an improvement on the initial ranking of 3.

They were also asked to rate the extent of the seriousness of the problem with which they were dealing—in this case, the problem of Arun's urge to offend. Darwin felt that this had improved, rating it at 4—in other words 'The problem is not that serious', whereas he rated it at 2.5 (serious to very serious) when the problem was first identified.

Arun, on the other hand, initially rated the problem at 5 ('It is not a problem at all'), even though it was he who identified the problem. In the final session, he rated it as 3 ('The problem is serious'), suggesting that the sessions had led him to believe that the urge to offend was a problem for him.

In the final session, Darwin and Arun were asked to comment on the general progress of the family since beginning the family work. Darwin felt that the family was getting along considerably better than when the counselling began, and that the one problem they most wanted help with was now much better. He also felt that the counsellors' 'attempts to understand what was happening in the family' and 'negotiating with Arun in the session' were particularly helpful. He thought the family work would help them to handle problems in the future.

Arun was also positive, although less so than his father. He felt that the family was getting on considerably better now than when they started the family work and that the one problem he most wanted help with was considerably better.

About six weeks after the family problem-solving sessions were completed, Darwin wrote an unsolicited letter to say thank you for the assistance he had received. He wrote:

> Before our involvement in family work I was in a bad way regarding how to cope with my son and his anger and offending. It was upsetting everyone around him. The family work helped us to develop strategies that assisted us both, and helped us talk to each other for the first time in many years . . . These sessions really helped . . . I am sure they would help other families too.

The co-workers felt that the intervention worked because the model provided the family with a lot of control over the direction of the sessions. They saw it as an empowering process in which the workers provided the structure but the clients did the work. Nevertheless, one of the workers was concerned that the clients' control over the process limited them to safe topics and that important issues such as Arun's relationship with his mother were not addressed.

The workers found the model particularly appropriate for the human services setting. Clients and families are often only involved with the agency for short periods, and the time-limited nature of the model is an advantage, as is its capacity to work with only two family members or the whole family. The model also seemed to work well in this setting because it encouraged family members to take responsibility for family problems rather than blame the offender.

Conclusion

This book stems from my own experience over many years working as a child protection worker, a probation officer, a foster care worker and a mental health worker. Despite five years of education in the human services, including family work training, when I first sat down to work with a family group I was uncertain about where to start and what to do next. In this book, I have tried to present a model that can provide human service workers with a set of skills and the confidence to work through a series of family work sessions with a client family. I am hopeful that, in turn, this will help to give opportunities for families in the human services—families who often have severely limited opportunities—to learn new skills and to develop better lives.

References

Ahmadi, K., Ashrafi, S., Kimiaee, S. & Afzali, M. (2010) Effect of problem-solving on marital satisfaction, *Journal of Applied Sciences* 10: 682–7.

Alexander, J., Barton, C., Shiavo, R.S. & Parsons, B.V. (1978) Systems behavioural intervention with families of delinquents: Therapist characteristics, family behaviour and outcome, *Journal of Consulting and Clinical Psychology* 44: 656–64.

Alexander, J.F. & Parsons, B.V. (1973) Short-term family intervention: A therapy outcome study, *Journal of Consulting and Clinical Psychology* 2: 195–201.

Andrews, D.A., Keissling, J.J., Russell, R.J. & Grant, B.A. (1979) *Volunteers and the One-to-One Supervision of Adult Probationers*, Ontario Ministry of Correctional Services, Toronto.

Andrews, D. & Bonta, J. (2003) *Criminal Psychology; Criminal Behaviour*, 3rd edn, Cincinnati, OH: Anderson Publishing Company.

—— (2010) *The Psychology of Criminal Conduct*, 5th edn, Newark, NJ: LexisNexis.

Andrews, D. and Dowden, C. (2005) Managing correctional treatment for reduced recidivism: A meta-analytic review of programme integrity, *Legal and Criminological Psychology* 10(2): 173–87.

Arnd-Caddigan, M. & Pozzuto, R. (2008) Use of self in relational clinical social work, *Clinical Social Work Journal* 36: 235–43.

Asen, E. (2002) Outcome research in family therapy, *Advances in Psychiatric Treatment* 8: 230–8.

Association for Family Therapy (2011) website, <www.family-therapy.org.uk>. Accessed 20 July 2012.

Attorney-General's Department (2007) *Family Counsellors in the Family Law System*, Australian Government, Canberra, <www.ag.gov.au/Families/Familyrelationshipservices>. Accessed 25 October 2011.

Baker, M.R. & Steiner, J.R. (1995) Solution-focused social work: Meta-messages to students in higher education opportunity programs, *Social Work* 40(2): 225–32.

Barber, J. (1995) Working with resistant drug abusers, *Social Work* 40(1): 7–23.

—— (2002) *Social Work with Addictions*, Palgrave Macmillan, Basingstoke.

Barnes, G. (1984) *Working with Families*, Macmillan, London.

Barton, C., Alexander, J.F., Waldron, H., Turner, C.W. & Warburton, J. (1985) Generalizing treatment effects of Functional Family Therapy: Three replications, *American Journal of Family Therapy* 13: 16–26.

Bateson, G. (1979) *Mind and Nature: A Necessary Unity*, New York: E.P. Dutton.

Berg, I.K. (1994) *Family-based Practice: A Solution-focused Approach*, W.W. Norton, New York.

Blow, A., Sprenkle, D. & Davis, S. (2007) Is who delivers the treatment more important than the treatment itself? The role of the therapist in common factors, *Journal of Marital and Family Therapy* 33(3): 298–317.

Boscolo, L., Cecchin, G., Hoffman, L. & Penn, P. (1987) *Milan Systemic Family Therapy Conversations in Theory and Practice*, Basic Books, New York.

Bourgeon, G., Bonta, J., Rugge, T. & Gutierrez, L. (2010). Technology transfer: The importance of ongoing clinical supervision in translating 'what works' to everyday community supervision, in F. McNeill, P. Raynor & C. Trotter (eds), *Offender Supervision: New Directions in Theory and Practice*, Willan, Abingdon, pp. 88–106.

Bowen, M. (1978) *Family Therapy in Clinical Practice*, Jason Aronson, Northvale, NJ.

Brown, J. (1997) Circular questioning and introductory guide, *Australian and New Zealand Journal of Family Therapy* 18(2): 109–14.

Burns, P. (1994) Pro-social practices in community corrections, unpublished Honours thesis, Department of Social Work, Monash University.

Carr, A. (2011) Thematic review of family therapy journals 2010, *Journal of Family Therapy* 33(4): 429–47.

Cheng, P.F. (2009) A narrative analysis of clinical social workers' use of self in the helping process: An exploration of Taiwan experience, *Dissertation Abstracts International* 70(3): 1031.

Cherry, S. (2005) *Transforming Behaviour: Pro-social modelling in Practice*, Willan Publishing, Abingdon, UK.

Compton, B., Galaway, B. & Cournoyer, B. (2005) *Social Work Processes*, 7th edn, Thomson Brooks/Cole, Belmont, CA.

Corcoran, J. (2000) *Evidence Based Social Work Practice with Families: A Lifespan Approach*, Springer, New York.

—— (2002) Developmental adaptations of solution-focused family therapy, *Brief Treatment and Crisis Intervention* 2: 301–14.

Corcoran, J. & Walsh, J. (2008) *Mental Health in Social Work: A Casebook on Diagnosis and Strengths-based Assessment*, Pearson/Allyn and Bacon, Boston.

Cuijpers, P., van Straten, A. & Warmerda, L. (2007) Problem-
solving therapies for depression: A meta-analysis, *European
Psychiatry* 22: 9–15.

de Shazer, S. (1988) *Clues: Investigating Solutions in Brief Therapy*,
W.W. Norton, New York.

Dewane, C. (2006) Use of self: A primer revisited, *Clinical Social
Work Journal* 34: 543–58.

Dowden, C. & Andrews, D.A. (2003) Does family intervention
work for delinquents? Results of a meta-analysis, *Canadian
Journal of Criminology and Criminal Justice*, 45(3): 327–42.

—— (2004) The importance of staff practice in delivering effective correctional treatment: A meta-analytic review of the
literature, *International Journal of Offender Therapy and Comparative Criminology* 48(2): 203–14.

Drummond, J., Fleming, D., McDonald, L. & Kysela, G. (2005)
Randomized controlled trial of a family problem-solving
intervention, *Clinical Nursing Research* 4: 57–80.

Elliot, F.R. (1986) *The Family: Change or Continuity?* Macmillan,
Basingstoke, UK.

Ellis, A. & Dryden, W. (2007) *The Practice of Rational Emotive Behaviour Therapy*, Springer, New York.

Epstein, N.B. & Bishop, D.S. (1981) Problem-centred systems and
the family, in A.S. Gurman & P. Kniskern (eds), *Handbook of
Family Therapy*, Brunner Mayel, New York, pp. 444–82.

Eysenck, H.J. (1959) Learning theory and behaviour therapy, *British Journal of Psychiatry* 105: 61–75.

Fischer, R. (2004) Assessing client change in individual and family
counselling, *Research on Social Work Practice* 14(2): 102–11.

Forgatch, M.S. & Patterson, G.R. (1989) *Parents and Adolescents Living Together. Part II: Family Problem-solving*, Castalia, Eugene, OR.

Freud, S. (1938) *The Basic Writings of Sigmund Freud*, Modern
Library, New York.

Goldenberg, I. & Goldenberg, H. (2008) *Family Therapy: An Overview*, 7th edn, Thomson Brooks/Cole, Belmont, CA.

Goodwin, V. & Davis, B. (2011) *Crime Families: Gender and the Intergenerational Transfer of Criminal Tendencies*, Trends & Issues in Crime and Criminal Justice 414, Australian Institute of Criminology, Canberra.

Gordon, D.A. & Arbuthnot, J. (1990) Promising approaches for chronic juvenile offenders: Interventions with the family and other social systems, paper presented at the annual convention of the American Society of Criminology, Baltimore, MD.

Gordon, D.A., Arbuthnot, J., Gustafson, K.E. & McGreen, P. (1988) Home-based behavioural systems: Family therapy with disadvantaged juvenile delinquents, *American Journal of Family Therapy* 16(3): 243–55.

Gough, D. (1993) *Child Abuse Interventions: A Review of the Research Literature*, HMSO, London.

Guevara, M. & Solomon, E. (2009) *Implementing Evidence-Based Policy and Practice in Community Corrections*, 2nd edn, US Department of Justice National Institute of Corrections, Washington, DC, <www.cjinstitute.org/publications/integratedmodel>. Accessed 20 November 2011.

Gurman, A.S. & Kniskern, P. (eds) (1981) *Handbook of Family Therapy*, Brunner Mayel, New York.

Haley, J. (1987) *Problem-solving Therapy*, 2nd edn, Jossey-Bass, San Francisco.

Harms, L. (2007) *Working with People*, Oxford University Press, Melbourne.

Hepworth, D., Rooney, R., Rooney, G., Strom-Gottfried, K. & Larsen, J. (2006) *Direct Social Work Practice*, 7th edn, Thomson Brooks/Cole, Belmont, CA.

Hoagwood, K., Burns, B., Kiser, L., Ringeison, H. & Schoenwald,

S. (2001) Evidence based practice in child and adolescent mental health services, *Psychiatric Services* 52(9): 1179–89.

Howe, D. (2010) The safety of children and the parent–worker relationship in cases of child abuse and neglect, *Child Abuse Review*, 19(5): 330–41.

Jones, J. and Alcabes, A. (1993) *Client Socialisation: The Achilles Heel of the Helping Professions*, Auburn House, Westport, CT.

Kim, J. (2006) Examining the effectiveness of Solution-Focused Brief Therapy: A Meta-Analysis, *Research on Social Work Practice* 18(2): 107–16.

Knott, C. & Scagg, T. (2010) *Reflective Practice in Social Work*, 2nd edn, Learning Matters, Exeter, UK.

Kolko, D. (2002). Child physical abuse, in J. Myers, L. Berliner, J. Briere, C. Hendrix, C. Jenny & T. Reid (eds), *The APSAC Handbook on Child Maltreatment*, 2nd edn, Sage, Thousand Oaks, CA, pp. 21–54.

Legal Services Commission of South Australia (2011) Website Glossary, <www.lawhandbook.sa.gov.au/go01.php#id4127712>. Accessed 10 October 2011.

Locke, B., Garrison, R. & Winship, J. (1998) *Generalist Social Work Practice: Context, Story, and Partnerships*, Brooks/Cole, Pacific Grove, CA.

Loneck, B. (1995) Getting persons with alcohol and other problems into treatment: Teaching the Johnson Intervention in the practice curriculum, *Journal of Teaching in Social Work* 11(1): 31–48.

Madanes, C. & Haley, J. (1977) Dimensions of family therapy. *The Journal of Nervous and Mental Disease*, 165(2): 88–98.

Malouff, J., Thorsteinsson, E. & Schutte, N. (2007) The efficacy of problem-solving therapy in reducing mental and physical health problems: A meta-analysis, *Clinical Psychology Review* 27: 46–57.

Mandell, D. (2008) Power, care and vulnerability: Considering use of self in child welfare practice. *Journal of Social Work Practice*, 22(2): 235–48.

Maruna, S. & LeBel, T. (2010) The desistance paradigm in correctional practice: From programs to lives, in F. McNeill, P. Raynor & C. Trotter (eds), *Offender Supervision: New Directions in Theory, Research and Practice*, Willan, Cullompton, UK.

Miller, S., Duncan, B., Brown, J., Sorrell, R. & Chalk, M. (2006) Using formal client feedback to improve retention and outcome: Making ongoing, real-time assessment feasible, *Journal of Brief Therapy*, 5(1): 5–22.

Minuchin, S. (1974) *Families and Family Therapy*, Harvard University Press, Cambridge, MA.

Morley, C. (2003) Critical reflection in social work: A response to globalisation, *International Journal of Social Welfare* 13: 297–303.

O'Hara, A. & Weber, Z. (2006) *Skills for Human Service Practice*, Oxford University Press, Melbourne.

Patterson, G.R. & Forgatch, M.S. (1987) *Parents and Adolescents Living Together. Part I: The Basics*, Castalia, Eugene, OR.

Perera, R. & Kathriarachchi, S. (2011) Problem-solving counselling as a therapeutic tool on youth suicidal behaviour in the suburban population in Sri Lanka, *Indian Journal of Psychiatry* 53(1): 30–5.

Perkins-Dock, R. (2001) Family interventions with incarcerated youth: A review of the literature, *International Journal of Offender Therapy and Comparative Criminology* 45(5): 606–25.

Perlman, H. (1957) *Social Casework: A Problem-solving Process*, University of Chicago Press, Chicago.

Polki, P., Ervast, S. & Huupponen, M. (2004) Coping and resilience of children of a mentally ill parent, *Social Work in Health Care* 39(1–2): 151–63.

Reid, W. (1985) *Family Problem-solving*, Columbia University Press, New York.

—— (1992) *Task Strategies: An Empirical Approach to Clinical Social Work*, Columbia University Press, New York.

—— (2000) *The Task Planner*, Columbia University Press, New York.

Reid, W. & Epstein, L. (1972) *Task-centred Casework*, Columbia University Press, New York.

Rex, S. & Maltravers, A. (1998) *Pro-social Modelling and Legitimacy*, University of Cambridge Institute of Criminology, Cambridge, MA.

Robinson, C., Vanbenschoten, S., Alexander, M. & Lowenkamp, C. (2011) A random (almost) study of staff training aimed at reducing re-arrest (reducing recidivism through intentional design), *Federal Probation*, September, n.p.

Rooney, R. (1992) *Strategies for Work with Involuntary Clients*, Columbia University Press, New York.

Rosen, D., Morse, J.Q. & Reynolds, C.F. (2011). Adapting problem-solving therapy for depressed older adults in methadone maintenance treatment, *Journal of Substance Abuse Treatment*, 40(2): 132–41.

Satir, V., Gomori, M., Banmen, J. & Gerber, J. (1991) *The Satir Model: Family Therapy and Beyond*, Science and Behaviour Books, Palo Alto, CA.

Selvini-Palazzoli, M., Boscolo, L., Cecchin, G. & Prata, G. (1970) Hypothesizing–circularity–neutrality: Three guidelines for the conductor of the session, *Family Process* 19(1): 3–12.

—— (1978). *Paradox and Counterparadox: A New Model in the Therapy of the Family in Schizophrenic Transaction*, Jason Aronson, Northvale, NJ.

Sexton, T. & Alexander, J. (2002a) Family based empirically supported interventions, *The Counselling Psychologist* 30(2): 238–61.

—— (2002b) Functional Family Therapy, *Juvenile Justice Bulletin*, n.d.: 1–8.

—— (2003). Functional Family Therapy: A mature clinical model for working with at-risk adolescents and their families. In T. L. Sexton, G. R. Weeks & M.S. Robbins (eds), *Handbook of Family Therapy*, Brunner-Routledge, New York, pp. 323–48.

Sexton, T. & Turner, C.W. (2010) The effectiveness of Functional Family Therapy for youth with behavioural problems in a community practice setting, *Journal of Family Psychology*, 24(3): 339–48.

Smokowski, P. & Wodarski, J. (1996) Effectiveness of child welfare services, *Research on Social Work Practice* 6(4): 504–23.

Spratt, T. & Houston S. (1999) Developing critical social work in theory and in practice: Child protection and communicative reason, *Child and Family Social Work* 4(4): 315–27.

Steib, S. & Blome, W. (2004) Fatal error: The missing ingredient in child welfare reform—part 2, *Child Welfare* 83(1): 101–4.

Stratton, P. (2005). *Report on the Evidence Base of Systemic Family Therapy*, Association for Family Therapy, <www.aft.org.uk/docs/evidencedocsept05creditedSS.doc>. Accessed 20 July 2012.

St Lukes Innovative Resources (2008) *Strengths Cards*, <www.innovativeresources.org/default.asp?cmd=product&productid=44233>. Accessed 20 July 2012.

Stuart, R. (1980) *Helping Couples Change*, Guilford Press, New York.

Taxman, F. & Bouffard, J.A. (2002) Assessing therapeutic integrity in modified therapeutic communities for drug-involved offenders, *The Prison Journal* 82(2): 189–212.

Trotter, C. (1990) Probation can work: A research study using volunteers, *Australian Journal of Social Work*, 43(2): 13–18.

—— (1996) The impact of different supervision practices in community corrections, *Australian and New Zealand Journal of Criminology* 29(1): 29–46.

—— (1997a) Working with mandated clients—a pro-social approach, *Australian Journal of Social Work* 50(2): 19–27.

—— (1997b) *Family Problem-solving*, Report to VicSafe, Department of Social Work, Monash University, Melbourne.

—— (1999) 'Don't throw the baby out with the bath water': In defence of problem-solving, *Australian Journal of Social Work* 52(4): 51–5.

—— (2000) Teaching family work: Integrating teaching practice and research, *Advances in Social Work and Welfare Education*, 3(1): 161–70.

—— (2002) Worker style and client outcome in child protection, *Child Abuse Review* 11: 38–50.

—— (2004) *Helping Abused Children and their Families*, Allen & Unwin, Sydney.

—— (2006) *Working with Involuntary Clients*, Allen & Unwin, Sydney.

—— (2010) Working with families in criminal justice, in F. McNeill, P. Raynor & C. Trotter, *Offender Supervision: New Directions in Theory, Research and Practice*, Willan, Cullompton.

Trotter, C., Cox, D. & Crawford, K. (2002) Family counselling in juvenile justice, *Australian Social Work*, 55(1): 119–27.

Trotter, C. & Evans, P. (2012) Analysis of supervision skills in juvenile justice, *Australian and New Zealand Journal of Criminology* 45(2): 255–73.

Trotter, C. & Ward, T. (2012) Involuntary clients: Pro-social modelling and ethics, *Ethics and Social Welfare* 6(2): 3–17.

Turner, S. (2010) Case management in corrections: Evidence, issues and challenges, in F. McNeill, P. Raynor & C. Trotter (eds), *Offender Supervision: New Directions in Theory, Research and Practice*, Willan, Cullompton, pp. 344–66.

UK Association of Family Therapists website, <www.aft.org.uk/home/familytherapy.asp>. Accessed 20 June 2012.

Videka, L. and Blackburn, J. (2010) The intellectual legacy of William J. Reid, in A.E. Fortune (ed.), *Advancing Practice Research in Social Work for the 21st Century*, Columbia University Press, New York, pp. 183–94.

Videka-Sherman, L. (1988) Meta-analysis of research on social work practice in mental health, *Social Work* 33(4): 323–38.

Wade, S., Taylor, H., Yeates, K., Drotar, D., Stancin, T., Minich, N. & Schluchter, M. (2006) Long-term parental and family adaptation following paediatric brain injury, *Journal of Paediatric Psychology* 31(10): 1072–83.

Whitaker, C.A. & Bumberry, W.A. (1988) *Dancing with the Family: A Symbolic-experiential Approach*, Brunner/Mazel, New York.

White, M. & Epston, D. (1989) *Narrative Means to Therapeutic Ends*, Dulwich Centre Publications, Adelaide.

Wilson, D. & Horner, W. (2005). Chronic child neglect: Needed developments in theory and practice, *Families in Society: The Journal of Contemporary Social Services* 86(4): 471–81.

Index